REMAINING TRUE

A biography of Ness Edwards

Wayne David

Published by the Caerphilly Local History Society

First published 2006

ISBN 0-9542782-1-6

Printed by Bruce Print
Alexander House, Graddfa Industrial Estate,
Llanbradach, Caerphilly, CF83 3QQ.

CONTENTS

ACKNOWLEDGEMENTS

Sincere thanks need to be recorded to the following: the family of Ness Edwards - his daughters Anne and Llin, his son Alan, his daughter-in-law, Olive, and his grandson, Keith; Alun Jones of St. Martin's School in Caerphilly; the enthusiasts of the Caerphilly Local History Society and the Bedwas and Trethomas Local History Group; the staff of the local libraries, particularly Bargoed, and of the South Wales Coalfield Collection at Swansea University; Dr. Hywel Francis MP; my members of staff; and all those people who supplied information and who agreed to be interviewed.

A special word of thanks must go to the **Barry Amiel and Norman Melburn Trust** for agreeing to give financial assistance to allow the book's publication.

To my late father, D. Haydn David,
whose love of history and commitment to the Labour Party continues to
inspire me.

FOREWORD

Ness Edwards was a 'man of the people' in every possible sense. Through his working class roots, his political ideology, his broad cultural and intellectual enthusiasm, his total commitment to the trade union movement, especially the South Wales Miners' Federation, his visionary internationalism and even in his love of rugby this remarkable man personified the essential nature of South Wales in its most tumultuous years. As Wayne David makes clear, to understand South Wales in the Twentieth Century, it is essential to comprehend individuals like Ness Edwards.

The MP for Caerphilly from 1939 until 1968 was very much a product of the coal mining community of South Wales. Gaining his education, experience, self-confidence and ever present optimism from the working class movement and its institutions, Ness was a critically important force in ending the pernicious Company Union in the South Wales coal industry before going on to play a central role in creating Britain's Welfare State. Alongside Aneurin Bevan and Jim Griffiths two better known South Walian giants of Labour - Edwards made a truly significant contribution to the Attlee Government's rescue of the British economy that had been battered by deep recessions, by war time damage, and by chronic underinvestment. He then went on to become the Post Office Minister who inaugurated radical change and modernisation.

He was not a man to mince his words, whether his targets were coal bosses, Moscow lackeys, the Welsh nationalists or those within the Labour Party who, as he saw it, were prepared to sell out democratic socialism. But although a politician and activist through and through, Ness Edwards - like many of his Labour movement contemporaries - was also a 'renaissance man' with a love of poetry, literature and music and a writing talent which, as his books and pamphlets demonstrate, was fluent and incisive.

Wayne David's book is a political biography which allows the humanity of Ness Edwards to shine through from start to finish. He does justice to his subject without being hagiographic; it is well researched and yet thoroughly readable. Those qualities should commend it to everyone who has an interest in understanding the history and the essential character of industrial South Wales, the Rhymney Valley, and the Labour movement as it grew from infancy to the greatness of Government.

2006 is the Centenary year of Labour Party representation in Parliament. There could be no better time for this outstanding book to be published, and to be read as a lucid reminder of the past and as an inspiration for the future.

Neil Kinnock

PREFACE

I first came across the name of Ness Edwards when I was a student at Cardiff University in the late 1970s. Two of Ness's books on the history of the South Wales miners were on a reading list for a Welsh History course taught by Professor Dai Smith. I remember being surprised that such erudite books had long been out of print and were, generally, so unappreciated.

The next time I really became aware of Ness Edwards was when I was elected the MP for Caerphilly 23 years later. Soon after my election I was asked by John Williams of the Caerphilly Local History Society if I would give a public 'talk' on an historical topic of my choice. I decided my subject would be 'Ness Edwards'. After carrying out a little research, encouraged by Ness's grandson, Keith, I became truly fascinated by Ness's eventful life. There was a large attendance at my talk and I was delighted that my enthusiasm was clearly shared by so many people in the Caerphilly area.

Shortly after, I decided to continue my research and write a short book on Ness's life. As I was warned, because of my Parliamentary commitments, the book took much longer to write than I anticipated. But, thanks to the assistance of a whole host of people, the book has finally seen the light of day and I am pleased it has appeared as the Labour Party is celebrating its Parliamentary Centenary.

Amongst my staff, Ben Curtis helped with research into hundreds of newspapers, Chris Bradley did lots of running around that defied any job description, and Marlene Rickards, as usual, was a source of good humour and unflappability and never complained about typing-up umpteen drafts. A huge thanks must go to the family of Ness who provided access to his papers, photographs and a tremendous amount of background information and advice. Not once was there anything other than complete support. Nor was there any suggestion that I should write a hagiography: this is a political history of a remarkable man; it is not an application for sainthood.

A special word of appreciation must be given to my friend and colleague, Dr. Hywel Francis MP, for reading the draft and offering helpful comments. My biggest debt of gratitude, however, is to the people of the Caerphilly constituency. Without the encouragement and assistance I have had from so many people in the Rhymney Valley, this 'project' would never have come to fruition. Ness Edwards considered it a great honour to be Caerphilly's Parliamentary representative. Today, I too feel equally honoured.

Wayne David
January 2006

CHAPTER 1

THE MAKING OF A WORKING CLASS LEADER

During his 71 years Ness Edwards was a radical working class intellectual, a prominent miners' leader, a reforming Government Minister, a trenchant opponent of Welsh nationalism and Communism and, during his last years, a respected elder statesman on the Labour backbenches. In many ways the story of Ness Edwards is the story of South Wales during its most tumultuous and defining years. It is also the story of a man who, in representing the people of the Caerphilly constituency for nearly 30 years, gave expression to the shared values of a mining community in the heart of the South Wales coalfield.

Ness was born in modest circumstances. On 5 April 1897, he began life in a terrace house in Castle Street, Abertillery, Monmouthshire. The second son of Ellen and Onesimus Edwards, Ness, too, was christened with the biblical name Onesimus*, but as a young man he was to formally change his name. Although Ness's father had come from a land-owning family in the Ebbw Valley in South East Wales, and his mother was the eldest child of a colliery under-manager, the family was far from prosperous. The modest wealth on his father's side, according to Ness's son, Rhys, had been "frittered away" by previous generations, leaving Ellen and Onesimus to bring up their children in circumstances typical of most Valley communities in the South Wales coalfield.

From an early age Ness experienced the harsh reality of life - and death - in a coal mining community. As a youngster, Ness witnessed his grandfather being brought home dead from the colliery at Six Bells after an accident. He was carried "on an old door - his body cloaked in a sheet of sacking". Ness's father, too, worked in the local colliery and had begun work at the age of eleven. His mother, Ellen, started work in a tin plate works in Ebbw Vale, when only nine, before moving to Nantyglo Iron Works. In his unpublished 'Brief History' of his father, Rhys Edwards wrote how his grandmother carried "iron ore in metal tubs" and "regularly came home with her hands cut and bleeding from this arduous task". In addition to her paid work, because her mother was ill, Ellen Edwards was also expected to "manage the family". This involved delegating various tasks to the

---

*Onesimus was a slave who escaped from his master and fled to Rome where he was converted to Christianity by the Apostle Paul.

other children but the most onerous of the weekly chores - the family wash - was her responsibility. Ellen was very short and to make this task possible Ellen's father made a box for her to stand on to reach the sink.

Ness's mother, although diminutive, was always a tower of strength. Like many working class women of her time, Ellen Edwards bore her hard life with fortitude, drawing inspiration from her non-conformist Christian beliefs. Her place of worship was the Blaenau Gwent Baptist Church in Abertillery, opposite which the family moved when Ness was a small boy. Having had no formal education, Ellen Edwards had taught herself to read and as her two eldest sons, William George and Ness, were growing-up she regularly read to them classics of English literature and, of course, the Bible.

At the Baptist Church the Minister was the formidable The Reverend Towy Evans. He was a well-known radical and, recognising that Ness had great potential, he soon 'took him under his wing'. Together they went to concerts at the Abertillery Co-operative Hall, and under the Reverend's guidance Ness developed a love for classical music and opera. Rugby also became one of Ness's great passions, an enthusiasm he maintained throughout his life.

Towy Evans and Ness's mother were the two big influences on the young Ness. It was, therefore, hardly surprising that Ness was baptised at the age of 15 and soon after became a Sunday School Teacher. It was also at this time, and through Christian teaching, that Ness began to develop an interest in politics. Increasingly, Ness considered the social message of Christianity. He became more and more aware of the need to translate the Christian message of the pulpit into practical measures of social change.

Like many of his contemparies, Ness's first taste of work was as a lather boy in a local barber's shop. After leaving the British School in Abertillery, his first 'real employment' came, at the age of 13, when he put on his new moleskin trousers, picked-up his water jack and tommy box for his food and walked three miles to the Vivian Colliery, Abertillery. Here he worked with his father and elder brother until their father became a Colliery Examiner at the Arrael Griffin No. 4 Pit at Six Bells. When Ness's brother, Billy, was given a stall at the Pit, Ness became his 'butty'.*

Many years later, in 1960, after an explosion at Six Bells Colliery in which 45 men lost their lives, Ness wrote in a national newspaper about his memories of working at Arrael Griffin No. 4. One of those memories was of a haulier losing his life in an accident. Once knowledge of the accident had spread amongst the colliers by men whispering one to another "all out, somebody killed," Ness recalled how "without talk, tools were put on the bar and we all made for pit bottom to wait our turn to go up". Such experiences left an indelible mark on Ness.

*A butty was an assistant in the mines.

2

After starting work, Ness was soon involved in the activities of the miners' trade union, the Federation, known by everyone as the 'Fed'. He regularly attended meetings of the Arrael Griffin Miners' Lodge (the branch) and was quickly elected its Chairman. As well as now taking a keen interest in the day-to-day well-being of his work mates, Ness became acutely aware of the great political and industrial debates which were now sweeping across the South Wales coalfield.

In 1912, the famous *'Miners' Next Step'* was published by the militants of the Unofficial Reform Committee. This was a pamphlet which drew heavily on syndicalist* ideas of workers' control, arguing for the Miners' Federation to be transformed into a rank-and-file organisation capable of bringing industrial democracy to the coal industry. A copy of the *'Miners' Next Step'*, with heavy pencil marks, is to be found in Ness's personal papers held by Baroness Llin Golding, one of Ness's daughters, and a reading of Ness's *'History of the South Wales Miners' Federation Volume 1'*, leaves one in no doubt that Ness saw the pamphlet as being of seminal importance. "In the history of trade unionism," Ness wrote, "no pamphlet has had such an effect as this pamplet had throughout the Country". Nor is the praise confined to the text. Having devoted an entire Chapter of his book to the *'Miners' Next Step'*, Ness concluded this section of his book with a huge tribute to the advocates of industrial democracy. He wrote, "No praise can be too great for the work this unofficial movement did in placing before the workers the principles contained in the *Miners' Next Step*".

These were the ideas and policies which had a profound influence on Ness as a young man. At the same time as he became active in his colliery lodge, Ness started to attend a study group at the local miners' institute. The group's tutor was George Dagger, a miner who was to become the Member of Parliament for Abertillery, and it was through him that Ness was drawn towards the Abertillery Branch of the Plebs League.

Established in October 1908, the Plebs League took its name from a pamphlet written by the American, Daniel de Leon, entitled *'Two Pages of Roman History'*. In the pamphlet, de Leon, the leader of the American Socialist Labour Party, outlined the struggle in ancient Rome between the property-owning patricians and the propertyless plebeians. The aim of the League was to stimulate interest in 'independent' working class education. Initially, the League began life in Ruskin College, the adult education College in Oxford, however following the formation of the break-away Marxist Central Labour College (CLC) in 1909, the League became the effective 'voice' of the Labour College in the country.

In the following years the Plebs League became the cutting edge of the independent working class movement, educating workers not for their own self-

---

* Syndicalist comes from the French 'syndic' meaning union.

3

improvement but so that they might play a role in emancipating their 'class'. The teachings of the Plebs League and the CLC were firmly rooted in the political ideology of Karl Marx and Marxist writers such as Dietzgen, Kautsky and Plekhanov but, significantly, they were also firmly wedded to the idea of industrial action and of working class control of industry as advocated by American 'syndicalists'. Daniel de Leon and the International Workers of the World, the so-called Wobblies, believed that workers' control of industry was the way to bring about socialism; political activity and local and national elections were at best an adjunct to the main struggle at the workplace. Power lay with the workers "at the point of production" or, as Noah Ablett, a Plebs League tutor in the Rhondda and one of the authors of *'The Miners' Next Step'*, put it "Why cross the river to fill the pail?"

In Abertillery and the western Valleys of Monmouthshire such ideas were well received. From different parts of northern Monmouthshire, young militants from the mines were being drawn to the Abertillery Plebs League meetings. One such militant was Myrddin Evans. He became a close friend of Ness and later held the position of Secretary of the International Labour Office. Another was the young Aneurin Bevan. Born in the same year as Ness, Nye shared many of Ness's developing views and, according to Rhys Edwards, Nye and Ness "spent hours in the front room" of Ness's parents' home discussing the likely political impact of the event that was soon to transform their lives - the First World War.

On the outbreak of hostilities in 1914 all the local members of the Plebs League took a pledge to oppose the war. Ness remained true to that pledge throughout the next four years. Despite the jingoistic mood which swept the country and the active pro-war stance of most of the Federation's leadership, Ness remained firmly committed to the anti-war movement and, if anything, his opposition became stronger as the bloody conflict dragged on. Supported by his mother and encouraged by members of the Plebs League, Ness joined the Non-Conscription Fellowship and, at about the same time, the Independent Labour Party (ILP).

Probably in 1916, when he received his 'call-up' papers, Ness absconded, eventually going to London and, according to his son, Rhys, Ness stayed in the home of an expatriate Russian Count. As the Russian's home at Hammersmith Broadway was under surveillance by the authorities, Ness was soon arrested and sent to Brecon barracks. Here he was harshly treated, being beaten and even chased naked around the barracks by soldiers with fixed bayonets.

Eventually, Ness appeared in front of a tribunal at which his 'conscientious objection' to the war was considered. Because Ness was an 'absolutist' and refused to take even a non-combatant role in the armed forces, such as becoming a stretcher-bearer, he was sent to Dartmoor Prison. On leaving the train at Princetown, near Dartmoor, Ness and the other conscientious objectors were

4

stoned by local children. In the prison their treatment was little better. Incarcerated in a small cell, in the same part of the prison as inmates with psychiatric problems, Ness and the other "conchies" were forced to work in the local stone quarries when the weather was good; when it rained they "picked oakum".*

Visits from the family were not allowed and on Friday the cell doors were locked at 5 pm, not to be opened again until Monday morning, in time for work. The only reading material allowed was the Bible.

Ness's son, Rhys, has suggested that on being transferred to Wormwood Scrubs from Dartmoor, Ness somehow escaped, probably by "jumping train". What is certain is that Ness escaped from his imprisonment in 1917 and, via a Jewish tailor's workshop in the East End of London, found his way to Llangynidyr Caves, near Brecon. Here he stayed for several months, maintaining contact with his political friends and family. However, the harsh weather conditions took their toll and Ness agreed to "come home to his mother", who then persuaded Ness to give himself up to the authorities. He then spent the remaining months of the war in Wormwood Scrubs.

At the end of the war, Ness was transferred to work in the Ewenny Quarries, near Bridgend, South Wales, and along with other conscientious objectors, he was placed in lodgings on the outskirts of the town. It was at this time that Ness met Elina Victoria Williams, his future wife. Elina was living and teaching in Bridgend and soon after they met she provided Ness with books, and probably financial assistance, so that he could continue his education.

Ness was told by the authorities that he would be returned to Wormwood Scrubs before his final release. The thought of returning to the 'Scrubs' filled Ness with dread and so, rather than face prison again, he absconded to the village of Kenfig Hill, about five miles west of Bridgend. He adopted the literary pseudonym of Dorian Grey and, with the help of Elina, he began to prepare in earnest for his entrance examinations for the Central Labour College in Earl's Court, London. Ness's elder brother, William, also made contact with William Brace, the miners' leader and MP for Abertillery, who had just been appointed Home Secretary, so that the way was smoothed for Ness's college entry.

From the beginning the Central Labour College was well-supported by the miners and, in the highly-charged post-war atmosphere it quickly became the recognised academy for young, working class militants. Its importance to South Wales cannot be over-estimated. As Ness himself wrote in later years, the CLC was the place from "Whence came the ideas that dominated South Wales in the first quarter of this [Twentieth] century". Again, in Ness's words "To the rebels of that generation,

*Old ropes were untwisted to use for sealing the seams of ships to make them watertight.

5

knowledge was power, and the only true place to get it was the London [Central] Labour College".

Now a 'free' man, in 1919 Ness sat two examinations for one of the six South Wales Miners' Federation (SWMF) scholarships to the College. Out of some 300 candidates, Ness came joint fourth. Also attending the College on Federation scholarships at the same time as Ness, were a number of Welsh miners who were to rise to become leading members of the British Labour movement. They included Len Roberts and his brother Bryn, the future General Secretary of the National Union of Public Employees, also from Abertillery; James Griffiths, a future President of the South Wales Miners' Federation and Labour Cabinet Minister, from the Anthracite District in west Wales; and Aneurin Bevan, from Tredegar, who was, of course, to be the future architect of the National Health Service.

Ness found arguing, debating and studying with such soul mates to be an exhilarating experience, even though one critic referred to them as "The Cocks" from "the dung fields of South Wales". Ness also enjoyed the cultural excitement of London. He visited art galleries and museums and made good use of the complimentary tickets to classical music concerts which were provided for the College's students. Ness also learned how to swim and play tennis, an activity not normally available to working class youngsters. Interestingly, Ness's period at the CLC gave him his first experience of electoral politics. In April 1921, a Parliamentary by-election was held in nearby Bedford and, although Labour's campaign was unsuccessful, Ness gave strong backing to the Labour candidate and was clearly enthused by the experience.

But study was the main purpose for attending the CLC and Ness was a good and earnest student. The three Volumes of Marx's *'Das Kapital'*, which Ness read in the College, are to be found in the Ness Edwards personal collection in the University of Wales, Swansea. Like many of the texts at the CLC, they were published by the Kerr publishing Company in Chicago, and provide an indication of the basis of the College's teachings. Fundamentally, the curriculum at the CLC was about bringing a "Marxian" perspective to bear on a wide range of subjects, including Industrial History and Philosophy. Certainly the study was intensive by any standards. In a letter, dated 15 November 1919, to a friend in Abertillery, Ness described the workload:

> *The week before last, essays on 'Forms of Value' and 'Error and Truth'. Last week, essays on 'Money and its Functions', which with me occupies only 20 pages. This week so far we have to criticise 'the hope of another world with its septernal happiness for disembodied spirits, brought about (in the Roman Empire) an indifference to the world and its material needs'.*

6

This will require a sketch of economic development of Rome and then ideological development. It will require about 6,000 words. In addition to this we have 2 and sometimes 3 lectures per day. On the 3rd Thursday in the month we have 4 lectures. This is intensive culture with vengeance.

On leaving the College Ness was full of a burning desire to change the world. Not only had his knowledge of 'scientific socialism' been extended but he had also developed new and important skills. He was now keen to put what he had learnt to good use and play a role in the Labour movement back in South Wales.

However, on his return to Abertillery, Ness found that he was 'black balled' for two years by the local coal owners. Finding it impossible to get work in any of the local collieries, Ness experienced periods of unemployment, interrupted by a number of short-term jobs. One of these was selling encyclopaedias from door to door.

As the economic climate of South Wales worsened during the 1920s, so the extra-parliamentary agitation of the population increased. One of the flashpoints of the early 1920s was at the Bedwellty workhouse. Here, in January 1923, 1,000 unemployed miners and their families, including a large number from Abertillery, marched on the Workhouse and kept the Board of Guardians* "imprisoned" for a day and a night. The aim of the protest was to secure an improvement in the rate of Poor Relief. Although there is nothing to confirm that Ness was actually involved in the "siege", there is no doubt that he was aware of it at the time and in the unpublished draft of his second Volume of the *'History of the SWMF'* there is a comprehensive account of the protest.

Still full of academic and revolutionary enthusiasm after the CLC, Ness became a tutor for the Plebs League and used much of this period of involuntary idleness to write a number of short books. Each was heavily influenced by what Ness had learned in the Labour College and were, in their different ways, notable and important works.

Ness's first book was *'The Industrial Revolution in South Wales'*. With a Preface, dated 29 July 1924, by A. J. Cook, the General Secretary of the Miners' Federation of Great Britain (MFGB), the book runs to over 100 pages. It gives a narrative of the industrialisation of the region and provides a clear Marxist analysis of the class divisions brought about by the "capitalist mode of production". The bibliography demonstrates the extent of Ness's reading. It also shows how Ness was breaking new ground by undertaking primary research to write a 'History of the People'. Among the Reports consulted were the *'First Report of the Commission of Enquiry into the Employment of Children and Young Persons in Mines and Collieries, etc.,*

*Until their abolition in 1929, the main function of the Boards of Guardians was to help the poor and destitute.

7

1841' and Home Office papers for 1800-1842. Ness also drew information from the *Cambrian Newspaper*, the *Merthyr Guardian*, the *Monmouthshire Merlin* and, what Ness called, "the Bloody Old" *Times*.

Because of this book the historian Gwyn A. Williams identified Ness as a true "organic intellectual" of the Welsh working class. He described Ness's book as one of the first serious histories of Wales and Gwyn A. Williams correctly pointed out that there had never before been anything like it and there was not to be anything like it for a generation. The book was, as Wales's greatest Marxist historian said, a "remarkable achievement". We should indeed "dig it up like the Republicans of the 1830s dug up Tom Paine". *

Ness's second book was *'The History of the South Wales Miners'*, published in 1926. The book begins with an account of the so-called "primitive syndicates" at the start of the industrial revolution and the narrative continues through to the Twentieth Century. In an 'Author's Note', at the start, Ness indicated that he intended to follow-up this book with a 'History of the South Wales Miners' Federation', which would "complete the story up to the present time".

In fact, Ness decided later to publish his *'History of the SWMF'* in two Volumes. The first Volume came out in 1938 and traced the Fed's development from its formation in 1898 until the mid-1930s. With a lucid and clear narrative it follows and explains all of the main developments and ideas which shaped the SWMF and, as such, it is truly a trail-blazing work, commanding an important place in Welsh Labour historiography. Until the publication of Robin Page Arnot's somewhat 'dry' *'History of the South Wales Miners, Volume 1'* in 1967, Ness's book was the only comprehensive history of the trade union which shaped South Wales in the first half of the Twentieth Century. As befits a socialist historian, Ness made clear in his Foreword that the book had a contemporary purpose:

> *the modern Welsh Miner will better assess the value of his trade union by knowing what tremendous tasks it has performed in the past ... the time may well come when even greater sacrifices will be necessary ... if this volume will assist in stimulating that preparedness to sacrifice, I shall be well pleased.*

Generally, Ness's book was well received. The one notable exception was a review in the Communist Party's paper *The Daily Worker*. The author was Idris Cox, District Secretary of the Communist Party in South Wales. Cox welcomed Ness's book but expressed his disappointment that Ness had not placed "on record the campaign of the leadership [of the Fed] against the militants from 1928 1933,

---

*Tom Paine was one of the founding fathers of the United States of America and the foremost radical of his time.

the campaign of the leadership [of the Fed] against the militants from 1928 1933, and the expulsion of Arthur Horner and others". In Cox's view this policy had reduced the SWMF "to a mere skeleton of its former self" and that only "when this policy was reversed" did the Federation rebuild itself.

Cox's review displays a bizarre distortion of history. From 1928 until 1933 the Communist Party had pursued its so-called 'Class against Class' policy. The Communists adopted an ultra-sectarian approach, condemning even 'left' Labour leaders as 'social fascists'. Contrary to what Cox argued, it was only when the Communist Party and Arthur Horner, the future President of SWMF, abandoned this policy did they regain influence and contribute to the rebuilding of the SWMF.

It is surely because Ness did not want to expose such acrimonious divisions within the Federation's recent past that he skirted over them in his writings. This is what Ness did in his first Volume History and, as all his notes indicate, what he intended to do in his second Volume.

Although trailed at the beginning and end of Volume 1 and written in draft and note form, Ness's second Volume of the Fed's history was never published. The reasons for its non-publication are touched upon in Chapter two and probably have more to do with legal sensitivities and time constraints than anything else.

Ness's *'History of the SWMF, Volume 1'* was, appropriately, published by the left wing publisher Lawrence and Wishart in 1938, with a special Left Book Club edition. Some years earlier, Ness's first two books were also published in London; the first by the National Council of Labour Colleges, and the second by the Labour Publishing Company Limited. Ness's third book, *'John Frost and the Chartist Movement in Wales'* was published by 'The Western Valleys Labour Classes, Abertillery, Monmouthshire', and printed locally, perhaps because some of the book had already appeared in *Plebs Magazine*. Ness's fourth and final book in this period was *'The Workers' Theatre'*. This was published in 1930 by the South Wales Miners' Federation's printers 'Cymric Federation Press', although the author's Foreword is dated August 1926.

Ness's books - on the Chartists and the *'Workers' Theatre'* - although lacking the depth and incisiveness of the later *'History of the SWMF'*, they are, nevertheless, powerful and important works. His work on the Chartist Movement relied on a mixture of primary and secondary sources and Ness wrote a good description of how the Chartists had bravely sought to promote the interests of working people. For Ness, John Frost, the leader of the Newport Chartists, "typified the best characteristics of the movement. A man who, in those days of heavy and cruel persecutions, was prepared to pay the heavy price of his life in uplifting the working class".

Yet, brave as the Chartists were, Ness concluded his short book by writing a classic Marxist explanation of why their actions were bound to fail. Ness believed that the Chartists would always have been defeated because "capitalist society with all its contradictions had not sufficiently developed". At the time of the Chartists, Ness believed working class control had simply not been possible.

In many ways Ness's book *'The Workers' Theatre'* is even more interesting. In the Foreword to the book, Ness explained that he had been "intentionally provocative". When writing this "little work", he stated that not only was he aware that many of the statements would shock the book's readers but many of his conclusions had even "shocked the author".

The book draws heavily on the arguments that Marxists were putting forward at the time to encourage a "proletarian culture" to help sustain and carry forward the revolutionary process in the fledgling Soviet Union and to promote revolutionary change elsewhere. Capitalist culture, including traditional drama, was in decline, it was argued, and had to be replaced by a new culture and drama based "on the character of the workers' movement". In the Introduction to the book, Ness confidently proclaimed that "while the capitalist class and its drama is essentially conservative, the new drama will be revolutionary in its message; it will echo the message of the modern working class movement".

In rejecting traditional bourgeois culture, Ness accused Shakespeare of dignifying royalty and making his plebeian characters figures of fun. He even criticised "a certain Welsh play" because it ended "with the singing of a funeral hymn". Sharp criticism was also directed at "well meaning middle-class intellectuals" who tried to take "good drama" to the workers. For Ness there could be no compromise; anti-working class drama, in all its forms, had to be rejected in favour of a workers' drama which would be uplifting and "a means of education, a mental stimulant". The end result would be new dramatic forms and expressions which would "intensify our enthusiasm and organise our feelings". This was, in the words of the historian Raphael Samuel, "the most systematic case for class struggle drama" written during the period.

Ness's early books were all relatively short and quite affordable for most miners. They were widely circulated across the coalfields but were particularly well read in South Wales, especially in the Plebs League discussion groups. These works, combined with Ness's lecturing and educational work, made his name well known throughout the Labour Movement.

Eventually, Ness had been able to gain employment again at his old colliery, the Arrael Griffin at Six Bells. Not surprisingly, within a short time Ness was elected to the Lodge Committee and in 1925 was re-elected as Chairman of the Committee, a position he had held before the war. During the same year he married Elina, with whom he had maintained close contact while in London. They married in Nolton Church, Bridgend, and set-up home in Abertillery. However, Elina's father, a County Court bailiff, vehemently disapproved of his daughter marrying Ness and refused to attend the wedding.

As a leading figure in the local miners' lodge, Ness played a key role in bolstering the resolve of both the miners and the broader community during the General Strike and lock-out of 1926. The struggle of that year was a defining moment for South Wales and for many of its younger leaders, including Ness. The events of that 'long, hot summer' demonstrated to Ness that industrial militancy, by itself, could not change society. The limitations of syndicalist ideas, which had so influenced Ness in his youth, were now very apparent.

In the winter of 1926, Ness began to put together 'rough notes' for a book he entitled *'A Rebel's Testament'*. Unfortunately, only the introduction and the first couple of paragraphs of the first Chapter, under the heading 'General Theory', were completed. Nevertheless, the few hundred words are interesting in a number of respects.

Although written in the third person, Ness's words were autobiographical. In powerful terms Ness described how he had changed his view of religion and of religious non-conformity. Now he saw the "Chapel" of his youth as a means through which the colliery official exercised influence. "The big men in the pit", he wrote, "were always the big men in the chapel". He particularly castigated the preacher who had supported the war effort and had prayed for the "punishment of God upon the wicked atrocity making Germans". After the experience of the Chapel, the CLC had meant a "process of wiping the mental slate clean ... and the task of the acquisition of a historical method and rules of correct thinking". This meant that "the gospel according to Marx replaced the tenets of little bethelism". As Ness grew older religion was to become increasing irrelevant; something which did not warrant hostility but, equally, something which could not be embraced either.

Throughout the text, the influence of the CLC is very evident. Typically, Ness argued that the demise of capitalism was inevitable, and that the "madness" of capitalism was the "dying tremors of an outworn system". And, paraphrasing Marx in the *'Communist Manifesto'*, Ness wrote that the "working class have nothing to lose but their poverty and insecurity, and a world to gain".

The purpose of the book was to have been, as Ness explained, "to lay the main trends ... behind the evolution of human society". An answer was promised to the question "whither Britain"? In 1926-27 Ness did not provide a definitive answer to his own question. The rough notes for the greater part of the book were not developed. This may have been because Ness himself, at this time, was not absolutely clear about how capitalism would be replaced. Or perhaps the practical imperative of rebuilding the Federation came to monopolise his time and energy.

11

CHAPTER 2

REBUILDING THE MINERS' FEDERATION

Ness's life changed dramatically in September 1927. Following in the footsteps of Bryn Roberts, who had been appointed a Miners' Agent in the Rhymney Valley, at the age of 30 Ness was appointed full-time Secretary of the Penallta Lodge of the Miners' Federation in the same valley. Penallta was one of the largest collieries in South Wales and in the aftermath of the General Strike and miners' lock-out the morale of the miners was poor and the organisation of the lodge at Penallta was lamentable. The local miners were crying-out for leadership and, in a short period of time, Ness proved that he was more than capable of meeting the huge challenge before him.

As the lodge Minutes indicate, Ness was a good organiser and he won the respect of his members by his evident diligence and conscientiousness. Much of Ness's time was spent pursuing individual cases on behalf of his members. Hundreds of cases received Ness's attention. They included pneumoconiosis and personal injury claims, appeals against disciplinary action and a wide range of disputes between his members and management. A high proportion of these cases were concluded successfully but, inevitably, some were not. One of these was the case of William Henry Broomhead of Wern Crescent, Nelson. For no less than 22 years Mr Broomhead had maintained a claim for a thumb injury. Although there was no hope of him winning his case, Mr. Broomhead wanted it pursued and Ness duly obliged. Such was Ness's commitment to his work.

Ness also impressed many outside of the mining fraternity. In a telling letter to Ness, now in the possession of Ness's grandson, Keith, a former officer at the Bargoed Employment Exchange recalled, many years later, Ness's knowledge of the detailed regulations governing unemployment benefit and Ness's effective work following the lock-out of 1926. It was this mastery of detail, combined with a dogged determination, which were to become two of Ness's hallmarks throughout his industrial and political life.

One of Ness's priorities was to rebuild the lodge membership, not least by organising regular 'show cards' at the colliery. In addition, he oversaw the local hospital and ambulance fund and ensured that the Penallta Lodge played its full

12

part in the democratic life of the Miners' Federation. Importantly, too, Ness made the lodge a real influence in the local community and the Labour Party. Financial support was given to the local Party and nominations were made regularly for elections to both the Board of Guardians and the Gelligaer Urban District Council (UDC).

In 1929, Ness himself stood successfully for the Local Authority. The Council was never as important for Ness as the Federation but, during his six years as a councillor he played a conscientious role in the work of the Authority, helping to establish the Council's reputation as a good provider of local services, particularly public transport.

Having won a good reputation for himself in Penallta, Ness was appointed a District Agent in 1932 and, when the Federation embarked upon a far-reaching re-organisation in 1933-34, Ness was confirmed as Miners' Agent for the new No. 6 Area, covering the Rhymney Valley and East Glamorgan Districts. Although the new Federation Executive Council (EC) was now a rank-and-file body, with Agents only able to sit in rotation and in an advisory capacity for two years, Ness was in a key position at a crucial time in the Federation's history. Also on the Executive, as an elected member for the No. 6 Area, was Ness's close associate, W. H. Crews. Over the next 35 years Bill Crews was to be Ness's closest friend and political confidant. Their strong personal bond was a powerful source of strength for Ness, not least during the traumatic and testing events which were looming.

For most of the 1930s Ness's life was dominated by one monumental issue the struggle against Company Unionism. Since the defeat of 1926, the South Wales Miners' Federation had faced sporadic challenges to its hegemonic influence over the South Wales coalfield. At Maesteg, in the Rhondda, at Nine Mile Point near Risca, and elsewhere, the South Wales Miners' Industrial Union (SWMIU), the so-called Non-Political "scab union", had threatened to displace the Federation. But the two major challenges in the South Wales coalfield were at the Taff-Merthyr Colliery, near the village of Bedlinog, and at the Bedwas Colliery, near Caerphilly. Ness Edwards played a pivotal role in both the Federation's campaigns against the SWMIU; both campaigns were successful and, as Hywel Francis and David Smith explained in *'The Fed a history of the South Wales Miners in the twentieth century'*, the hard won victory at Bedwas, following as it did the success at Taff-Merthyr, "paved the way ... for the final elimination of scab unionism from the South Wales coalfield".

In the aftermath of the General Strike, the Taff-Merthyr Steam Coal Company Limited opened a new pit near Bedlinog. From the outset there was a determination by the Company to recognise the SWMIU rather than the Federation. Initially, the employers and their favoured union had a large measure of success; in July 1930, for example, the local Miners' Agent, S. O. Davies, lamented the fact that the Federation might have no alternative but "to abandon that Colliery to the tender mercies of the 'Non-Pols'".

After its internal re-organisation, the Federation decided that the time was right to mount a determined campaign. Ness Edwards, now the Agent for the new No. 6 Area, and Bill Crews, the EC member, were both acutely aware that in the event of a major industrial stoppage the Rhymney Valley was facing the prospect of having, on its doorstep, two 'Non-Pol' union pits undermining its resolve. In the autumn of 1934 the SWMF Executive acted: Ness Edwards and Bill Crews were placed in charge of the Taff-Merthyr and Bedwas campaigns, with Taff-Merthyr being given priority. At the same time Arthur Horner, a prominent Communist and Miners' Agent from the Anthracite District, was "unofficially" drafted to the area to mobilise local militants. Other officials and EC members were similarly deployed. There were to be key people in each of the main villages from which the Taff-Merthyr workforce was drawn   Trelewis, Nelson and Bedlinog. Ness described why this was necessary and how the campaign began in earnest:

> *The long valley from Nelson right up to Dowlais was a wilderness from an organisation point of view. We canvassed the idea of forming an Unemployed Lodge in Bedlinog, and eventually W. H. Crews and myself made a report to the EC which gave permission to establish the Lodge, subject to the agreement of the Dowlais Lodge. This was obtained, and on Friday, 21 September, we called a meeting of the Unemployed and set up the Taff Merthyr Lodge (Unemployed). The meeting appointed a Committee and Officers, and these were given the task of distributing the Non-Pols' Balance sheet, which we had ready in leaflet form, with a critical commentary. This had already been done at Bedwas. These leaflets were distributed that day. The base had been formed and the attack commenced. The battle for Freedom had commenced.*

The Federationists in the Unemployed 'Lodge' actively distributed leaflets to the men at the pit, held evening meetings in the villages, visited every man "except Company stooges", and brought in a loudspeaker mounted on a car for use at both the pit and in the villages.

The Company Union responded to this last action by using a heavily boarded lorry with a radiogram and a powerful amplifier, and the Company itself used electric hooters to drown-out Federation speakers whenever they began to address colliers near the pit. More importantly, the Company redoubled its efforts to bring in new 'blackleg' workers.

To begin with, the Federation's campaign went very well. At a mass meeting on a steep mountainside above the colliery over 200 men joined the Federation and in the villages it was a similar story, with 200 men in Bedlinog alone paying their dues. "But the Federation campaigners", wrote Ness, "had underestimated the length to which the Company Union would go". In Bedwas the 'Non-Pols' became far more aggressive towards the Federation and in Taff-Merthyr "flat-nosed, cauliflowered-eared thugs and touts" were now working hard to intimidate the Federationists. In one incident, at midnight "a new Ford 8 car rushed to a home in Bedlinog where two Executive Council members … were staying for the night. Shop windows on the ground floor were smashed in with two flagons. The car then rushed through Bedlinog in the direction of Taff-Merthyr colliery".

The owners' most dramatic reaction to the SWMF campaign came on 12 October when the men who had joined the Federation were threatened with dismissal. The men receiving those threats demanded the support of the Federation; they were not disappointed. Jim Griffiths, the new President of the SWMF, and Arthur Jenkins, the Vice President, gave immediate support to industrial action at the colliery and each striker was granted strike pay from Federation funds.

For nine weeks 1,100 Taff-Merthyr miners, out of a workforce of 1,500 went on strike "for the right to join the Federation". A bitter conflict ensued. At the start of the strike between 100 and 250 were at work, despite heavy picketing and hostile receptions for the strike breakers when they returned to their home villages. The *Western Mail* reported that a new tactic was now being used in the communities. As 'scabs' were walking down a street, large crowds, including many women, on both sides of the street stood in silence and doffed their hats and caps as if acknowledging a funeral.

During the following weeks there were indications that social tensions were now becoming acute. There were suggestions that Church and Chapel services attended by 'Non-Pol' members would be boycotted; Nelson Welfare AFC had resignations from its SWMIU committee members and even a local Silver Band and a Male Voice Party faced disruption because of serious divisions. Increasingly, those associated with the Company Union faced social ostracism. In Bedlinog, milkmen, shopkeepers and bakers with links to the SWMIU were boycotted and in Nelson, a barber whose son was a member of the Industrial Union saw his trade plummet. The depth of feeling could also be gauged from the fact that 'scabs' had their windows smashed and had tar daubed on their doors during the night.

Such actions were not part of the Federation's campaign. Central were the mass meetings held throughout the area and, as Ness explained, the huge torchlight procession from Bedlinog to Treharris "lit-up the coalfield in more ways than one".

Real tension was always present and one of the main reasons for this was the actions of the Glamorgan Constabulary which, it would seem, adopted a far more vigorous approach than its counterpart in Monmouthshire. On one occasion, summonses were issued against over a dozen miners' officials, including Ness, for alleged unlawful assembly and intimidation of a 'blackleg'. But when the case was heard at the Swansea Assizes, it was abruptly cut short. The judge declaring that "it would have been a great grief to him if it had been found necessary to record a conviction against any one of the men for what had happened". Ness recorded that the consternation on the face of Captain Lionel Lindsay, the Chief Constable of Glamorgan, was "remarkable to behold". Others, however, were less fortunate. In 1936, following disturbances at Bedlinog, 52 men and three women were convicted and some received as much as 15 months hard labour.

Despite the overwhelming majority feeling in these villages in support of the Federation, a hard-core of Company unionists continued to work. A number of these 'blacklegs' came from some distance away but others were relatively local. Ness explained why:

> *In the derelict northern end of the Rhymney Valley, the poor despairing unemployed miner would see glimpses of rolls of pound notes, "which we can get with your Union at Taff". In the Merthyr area the same tactic 'subs' of 25s. and free transport. A Guarantee of employment and the pick of the work. The chance of a lifetime as against the black bitter despair of the derelict area. Steal another man's job, become a tool of the Company, rat on your fellow workers; forget your tradition, remember your own kids want boots and clothes; get drunk and become a blackleg. The policeman will save you from the desserts which you know rightly belong to you. Such was the individual drama.*

Because of a small number of men continuing to work at the colliery, and more importantly, the total refusal of the local management, or directors of the parent companies, to meet with Federation officials, by November 1934 it was clear that the Federation had no option but to threaten an escalation of the dispute. The alternative was certain defeat. On 7 November delegates to a coalfield-wide conference agreed to give 14 days notice of industrial action.

The tactic worked. The Company changed its stance and negotiations soon began. The Federation postponed the tendering of notices and a negotiated settlement was reached. In his notes for his second Volume of the *'History of the South Wales Miners' Federation'*, Ness gave a clear summary of the agreement:

> *... employment at the colliery was limited to ex-Taff-Merthyr men on the basis of seniority. The Company union agreement was cancelled, and the employers bound themselves never again to deduct contributions from wages for the Company union. The final choice of the union to be recognised was to be decided by a ballot vote of the workmen.*

16

In the circumstances, the agreement was a clear success. Although a compromise, it did give the Federation real gains. But perhaps more important than the agreement itself was the fact that the Fed was able to mount a sustained campaign over many months, demonstrating that it was on the way back. As Ness put it "The campaign … was the best tonic that the Welsh miners had had since 1926". The campaign was, of course, the responsibility of Ness Edwards. He had been deputed by the SWMF Executive to organise such a campaign and he had done it well.

The agreement at Taff-Merthyr was not appreciated by everyone. Many men had effectively lost their jobs as a result of the agreement and local Communist Party activists were vocal in their condemnation. Throughout the campaign at Taff-Merthyr there had been a tension between Ness Edwards, the 'organiser', who some saw as being brought in from outside, and the local militants who had been 'chipping away' since 1926, albeit with little success.

These tensions came to a head in two acrimonious Taff-Merthyr lodge meetings in Bedlinog in January 1935. Both meetings were called to consider the terms of the negotiated agreement. At the first meeting, Ness replied to a number of questions regarding how the terms of the settlement were to be carried out, making the point that the negotiations had been conducted in accordance with the constitution of the Miners' Federation of Great Britain. But he made it plain that, as reported in the *Merthyr Express*, "he strongly resented the interference of a certain political party (the Communists) in the dispute, and so long as he was Agent for the District he would not allow any political party to dictate to him. Bedlinog was the only place in the District where Party strife was introduced into an individual dispute".

At the next lodge meeting, a fortnight later, things became personal. At the meeting Ness was invited to give his views on the agreement but he declined to do so because of the presence of Councillor Edgar Evans. He was a Communist Party member of Gelligaer UDC and an iron-monger in Bedlinog whose shop had been 'attacked' earlier by Company "thugs". Ness pointed out that Councillor Evans had no right to be in the meeting as he was a tradesman, and not a miner, and that "whilst he was Agent he was not going to allow any Communist to interfere in matters concerned with his work". As Edgar Evans refused to leave the meeting, Ness sat down. Uproar ensued as lodge members and Edgar Evans's supporters argued with each other. "Eventually", according to the local newspaper, "the stand-off ended with Ness having stuck to his guns and the Communist section withdrawing".

Despite the opposition of the local Communists, the negotiated agreement was accepted by the Taff-Merthyr workforce. The Fed had received a modest but vitally important fillip. The scene was now set for Ness to give his undivided attention to the other 'Non-Pol' colliery in the area.

Bedwas, and the neighbouring village of Trethomas, were relatively recently developed mining communities. With the sinking of the first Bedwas pit in 1911, large numbers of colliers migrated from the valleys of northern Monmouthshire, bringing with them a strong trade union tradition. This was, after all, the area where the early trade union movement, known as Scotch Cattle, and Chartism had their roots.

From the outset the miners had secured good terms and conditions, and the Instone brothers of the Bedwas Navigation Colliery Company (1921) Limited, had gained a reputation as good employers and generous patrons of the Bedwas Workmen's Hall, one of the finest in South Wales. However, this was before the coalfield, and the Company in particular, slipped into economic crisis.

The benevolence of the Company dried up as the price of coal steadily fell in the early 1920s and, by 1927, the owners were becoming increasingly determined to introduce measures to enhance the Company's profitability. In 1928 the miners were obliged to accept a significant reduction in the price list but further wage cuts were insisted upon. Disagreements between the owners and the lodge led to lock-outs in 1928 and 1930, and throughout 1931-32 disputes were erupting continually. The management now brought in contractors, employed 'strangers' rather than local men, put boys in place of men to work on the screens to sort the coal, and, on at least one occasion, even requested that some men work on May Day.*

Traditionally, the Bedwas Lodge had been fiercely independent of the SWMF as a whole and late in 1932 the men at Bedwas decided to strike without securing the support of the SWMF Executive. Ness had just become the new District Agent and had reservations about the wisdom of this move, believing that the men "had walked into the trap" set by management.

Once the strike had been declared, the Company were out recruiting 'blacklegs'. As Ness explained, "The Halt, lame and rejects of industry were persuaded with "pints" and bribes to go to Bedwas. Men who had had "Lump Sums" for injuries in other pits, and therefore had no hope other than this of getting back to the pit, saw their chance". Then, in February 1933 the Company 'took the plunge' and formally recognised the SWMIU.

The very week the strike began 300-400 men were "imported" and mysteriously a photograph of a Company document came into Ness's hands indicating the policy of management. The numbers of 'blacklegs' grew and a delegate Conference of the SWMF voted to advise all lodges across the coalfield to tender 14 days' notice in support of the Bedwas men. But when the SWMF EC received feed-back from the coalfield it saw a bleak picture. Partly because of long standing antagonisms

*May Day is the traditional international workers' day, now a Bank Holiday.

18

between the Bedwas Lodge and its Secretary, and the SWMF, there was, at best, only lukewarm rank-and-file support for action across the coalfield. In these circumstances, the EC had little option but to cancel the tendering of notices.

At the same time, large numbers of police had been moved into the Bedwas, Trethomas area. The Company provided two wooden barracks, where over 50 members of the Monmouthshire Constabulary were stationed under the command of Superintendent Spendlove. Their purpose was to ensure that the growing number of 'blacklegs', from as far afield as Brecon and Sennybridge, Cwm and Llantwit Fardre, as well as from the locality, were able to gain access to the colliery. On each of the colliery's entrances, however, there were hundreds of pickets consisting of members of the local community, especially women, as well as members of the lodge.

On Friday, 17 March a stone throwing incident occurred and, as a consequence, extra police reinforcements were brought in. Then, on the following day, a major confrontation occurred. John Davies, a 'scab', who walked with the aid of a stick, was being accompanied by the police, some of whom were on horseback, from the pit back to his home in Coronation Street, Trethomas. A large crowd gathered around them and "a part of a brick" was thrown, hitting John Davies on the side of his head and causing him to collapse. Several police officers went into the crowd and seized two women, Mrs Emily Parry and Mrs Mary Ludlow. The women were then "escorted" in the direction of Bedwas Police Station but the police stopped outside Bedwas Workmen's Hall and bundled the two women into an empty council bus parked outside. The terrified bus driver, however, scrambled from his cab taking the ignition key with him. Hearing the commotion outside, the lodge Secretary, W.J. Milsom, came out of the hall and saw a sergeant and another policeman holding Mary Ludlow down in between two seats. Milsom pleaded with the policemen to allow 'him' to accompany the two women to the Police Station. The sergeant replied that he had his orders and he had to carry them out. The police then continued with their distressed and dishevelled "prisoners" towards Bedwas Police Station. All the way they were followed by an angry and constantly growing crowd led by W. J. Milsom. By the time the procession had reached the police station there were at least 1,000 in the angry crowd calling for the women to be released.

Although the lodge officials attempted to calm the crowd, it seems that again a stone was thrown, hitting a policeman. Possibly fearing that the crowd would storm the Police Station, the police called a local Justice of the Peace to read the Riot Act. Edgar Lewis arrived, read the Riot Act and then the police "waded into the crowd, hitting out in all directions". Ness wrote that the police batoned old men, women and other innocent onlookers "with zest". The result was that, within a few minutes, the crowd was dispersed and the main street (Church Street) was left strewn with the injured.

According to newspaper reports, the "riot" had left six policeman and 20 others injured. 100 Summonses were heard at Caerphilly Police Court, with charges including stone throwing, the use of indecent language and obstruction. The majority of those charged were fined, but 24 people were sent to Monmouthshire Assizes accused of "riotously assembling at Trethomas and Bedwas on March 18 and did make great riot and disturbance to the terror and alarm of His Majesty's subjects". At the trial, the prosecution was unable to call any civilian witnesses and instead relied entirely on police evidence. All the defendants were defiant and unrepentant about their role in the disturbances. Goff Price, husband of Lillian May Price, a Communist and a future member of the International Brigade in Spain, stated that he had no apology for calling a man a 'scab'. If a man "takes your tools", said Goff Price, this is what he is. Lillian Price was equally unrepentant, although her involvement was marginal. She told the Court that she had called the workmen "scab and blackleg" because she wanted to shame them.

Another defendant, well known to the police, was Jack Roberts from Abertridwr. Jack Roberts, or Jack 'Russia', as people in the locality called him, had appeared in Court on numerous occasions and he boasted that he had paid enough money in fines to shoe the whole of the Glamorgan Constabulary. He was a staunch Communist and he, too, was shortly to volunteer to fight in Spain with the International Brigade.

Richard Felstead, in his biography of his grandfather, 'No Other Way', described how Jack Russia had set out on a borrowed bicycle to sell Communist Party raffle tickets in Nantgarw on the morning of 18 March. Wearing a pair of "fashionable Harris Tweed plus-fours and an open-necked khaki shirt" Jack Russia pedalled to the foot of the steep Cwrtrawlin Hill, got off his bicycle and began to push. But it was cold and the wind was blowing in his face, so Jack had second thoughts. He decided to cycle instead to the east of Caerphilly and the villages of Bedwas and Trethomas. His intention was to observe how the villagers were receiving the 'blacklegs' as they came off the morning shift.

Apparently, Jack Russia arrived at Trethomas at 2.30 pm and joined the crowd at the gates of the Bedwas Colliery. At 3.00 pm four blacklegs, with a police escort, left the colliery, before attention focussed on the blackleg John Davies. Jack Russia then moved along with the crowd as it came down Navigation Street and, as the Police Officers who had arrested the two women protesters were followed, he witnessed what happened outside the Bedwas Workmen's Hall and continued with the crowd to Bedwas Police Station. When outside the Police Station, Jack Russia stood in the middle of the road with the rest of the crowd. In the police charge Jack was caught a glancing blow across the shoulders. He stumbled into the gutter, regained his balance and escaped from the scene. Some days later, however, Jack Russia was summoned to appear in the local Police Court. From there he was sent, with the other 23, to appear at Monmouthshire Assizes.

At the end of the trial, after the jury had deliberated for an hour and a quarter, Mr. Justice Lawrence passed sentence. Of the 24 accused, seven men and four women were sentenced to between one and six months. Jack Russia received six months. The sentences were to be served in Cardiff Gaol.

As the prisoners were being led away to the cells, Lil Price shouted "down with fascism! Three cheers for the Bedwas strike. We cannot get justice". Before the trial she had displayed her five summonses in her front window because she was "bloody proud" and at the start of the trial she had refused to take the religious oath because of her commitment to Communism. For many, Lil Price personified the spirit of the whole conflict. Years later, Lil Price was interviewed by the historian Hywel Francis and she explained just how peripheral her involvement in the fracas had been:

> ... I was going out shopping, I had my little boy with me. He was only three years old and somebody said to me [that] the policeman was standing at the bottom of the street. They knew I wasn't in the baton charge because they were guarding the house where one of the scabs was living, and I spoke to him as I passed.

This was the most serious community confrontation in South Wales in the struggle against Company Unionism. The strength of feeling in the local community is difficult to exaggerate with the social and political fractures going deep. Recollections of the disturbances still abound. For example, the local historian, Glyndwr G. Jones, colourfully recalled his father's involvement in the disturbance. He had been a striking miner at Bedwas and was so incensed by the actions of the mounted police that he:

> ...returned home for his garden fork. On his return to the colliery the police once more charged the crowd. This time my father was waiting and he is supposed to have stuck his fork into the flanks of the horse thus unseating the policeman. The police retaliated and my father was brought home on a stretcher. This was my first sight of gore.

The riot at Bedwas and the subsequent trial attracted widespread attention. In the House of Commons, Charles Edwards, the Labour MP for Bedwellty, within whose constituency Bedwas was situated, secured an Adjournment Debate on the dispute and made one of his rare Parliamentary contributions. In his speech he pleaded the case for his constituents. He gave an overview of the background to the disturbances and praised the "restraint" of the crowd. If a stone had indeed been thrown, Charles Edwards said, such was the provocation that "it is a wonder there was not a volley of stones".

Then Charles Edwards turned to address the sentences received by the defendants. The sentences were "harsh, cruel and unjust", imposed on decent people who could not help protesting. Their crime, said the MP for Bedwellty, was simply trying to protect their jobs, their homes and their children. Some of those small children were now being looked after by friends and neighbours as their parents were incarcerated in prison. One of the men had four children and a wife who was suffering from tuberculosis. It was blatantly unfair, claimed Charles Edwards, that the same Court which gave sentences of six months imprisonment to some of the Bedwas defendants, on the same day, gave only a twelve month suspended sentence to a man from Monmouthshire, who had systematically defrauded people of thousands of pounds over a period of two years. Charles Edwards had already met the Home Secretary to discuss the Bedwas cases, now he publicly called on him to intervene and reduce the sentences. Charles Edwards pleaded that if ever there was a case for sympathetic consideration "this is one".

In the Debate, Charles Edwards was followed by Morgan Jones, MP for Caerphilly. In the short time available to him, Morgan Jones eloquently described to the House the situation in Bedwas. He began by telling his colleagues how his own relatives on his grandfather's side had come from Bedwas when it was a very small village. Now, Morgan Jones described it as "a comparatively big modern mining township", dependant however upon only one colliery. It was towards this one and only employer that people gravitated in their thousands, with the Company even building houses for the miners so as to encourage people to move to the area. Having thus enticed thousands of people from all over South Wales to Bedwas, Morgan Jones asked the House if it was fair for the Company then to issue an "edict" that no one from the area should in future be employed at the colliery. MPs were also asked to bear in mind that there was absolutely no alternative employment in the area.

This was the first point Morgan Jones made; the second was about how the people of Bedwas had felt when labour was imported from afar. In passionate terms Morgan Jones directed his comments at the Home Secretary. Morgan Jones asked how he would feel if:

> *he were in the position of an unemployed man who saw a colliery Company wilfully bringing hundreds of people a dozen miles, to work at the pit where he had earned his livelihood before and where he was forbidden to earn it any longer? In such circumstances would not the Rt Hon Gentleman feel hurt? Would he not feel bitter and angry about it? Would he not, perchance, find it impossible to call these people who were supplanting him and thousands of his fellows, by the name of "blacklegs"? But in this case the people for whom we are appealing were haled [sic] before the courts for shouting the word "blacklegs" at those who had been brought in to take their places.*

The riot in Bedwas served to bolster dramatically the resolve of the local colliers in their struggle. This was class conflict in its undiluted form. But the Bedwas miners' mood was in contrast to that of the rest of the coalfield. Here there was little appetite for a confrontation with the coal owners. Reflecting this reality, the Federation EC decided that the Bedwas men ought to return to work. This meant the Industrial Union and the Company had secured a major victory. As Ness recorded accurately, the EC decision meant that "The Industrial Union which had come to Bedwas as a strike-breaking machine" now "was installed as a partner in industrial co-operation".

Once the strike had collapsed, the majority of Federation men now found themselves without work. By the middle of 1933 the SWMIU had recruited 1,300 blacklegs, working on lower wages and poorer conditions. This was adding insult to injury, and local tensions reached fever pitch. The local community was now even more bitterly divided with virtually every family in the area being affected one way or another. From the Chapels to the Rugby Club there was friction. The men who had joined the scab union even found it necessary to establish their own separate social club in Navigation Street - the Ruperra Club.

The implications of the management's decision to rely on imported scab labour were far-reaching. Those miners who had bought their homes were unable to keep up the repayments and were facing huge debts; local shopkeepers were staring at financial ruin; men were beginning to look for work outside of South Wales. The scale of the local crisis was best summed-up by the Clerk to Bedwas and Machen UDC when he stated publicly that if the management of the colliery persisted in giving employment only to men outside of the area, "then such a policy could have only one result bankruptcy and ruin for the district and all concerned in it". He estimated that there were now only 50 out of a workforce of 1,500 who were from the Bedwas area, and if such a situation continued it would mean that it would be impossible for the local authority to meet its "heavy financial commitments".

Not content with displacing the Federation from the colliery, the MIU now began to 'flex its muscles' on the Board of Management of the Miners' Hospital in Caerphilly. In 1934, there was a concerted attempt to increase the number of Industrial Union Representatives on the Board in "contravention" of the rules of the hospital and against the interests of Federation members, not only in Bedwas, but in all the surrounding collieries.

Throughout 1934 and 1935 Ness led a relatively low key campaign to win over the miners at Bedwas but it was not until 1936 that the Fed felt that the time was right for a real fight back. Early that year, Arthur Horner, a prominent Communist, was elected President of the SWMF, succeeding Jim Griffiths, when he was elected Labour MP for Llanelli. Horner visited Bedwas and emphatically declared that "Scab Unionism is fascism in embryo". The plans which had already been drawn up for confronting the Company and its union were operationalised and Ness Edwards and Will Crews were given the responsibility of organising the campaign. What unfolded was the most determined and best organised campaign the coalfield had seen.

In the unpublished draft of his second Volume of the *'History of the SWMF'*, Ness explained that "Through an intermediary, contact was made with … two Industrial Union officials who had been dismissed from Bedwas. For certain inducements", wrote Ness, "a substantial quantity of Company Union documents passed into the hands of the Federation officials". One of the MIU officials was then "induced" to allow the publication of a leaflet with his name attached. The leaflet read as follows:

> *Corruption - Victimisation - Double dealing - Collusion - Bribery; these are the themes of a story of filth in the South Wales coalfield which will be unfolded to you within the forthcoming weeks.*
>
> *Coalowners, Public men, Members of Parliament, Peers, and others will figure prominently in these disclosures.*
>
> *Within this plot to deprive British workmen of their right to belong to a legitimate trade union the Company union has its place. The thread of this plot moves from the Coalowners to the Company union, from the Company union to MPs; from the Houses of Parliament through the Conservative Party; from the Conservative Party to country seats of coalowners; from these residences to the Coalowners' Association; from a Coalowners' Association to a English Company union; and back through this Company union to Taff Merthyr and Bedwas.*
>
> *Behind the fabric of British society, with the connivance of legal institutions, a plot has been hatched which would make a fitting theme for an Edgar Wallace thriller.*

According to Ness, the documents which the Federation obtained also "led to the termination in office of a high Police official who had always been known for the zeal which he brought to the persecution of Federation men".* In addition, they explained the ease with which "Company Union thugs" were able to carry out their intimidation.

The information in these documents was used to good effect. During the next few weeks a leaflet was produced nearly every day by Ness, either in the name of the

*Presumably this was a reference to the infamous Lionel Lindsay, the long standing Chief Constable of Glamorgan, who retired at the end of 1936.

SOUTH WALES MINERS' FEDERATION.

To the Miners who are Robbed of the Right to Organise.

The Industrial Union is the British form of Fascism. Its tactics contain all the element of the Hitler regime.

Its first tactic is to destroy the free Trade Union, and establish, by terrorism, a little group of strangers who are imposed on the men as its spokesmen. Their wages are obtained by compulsory deduction from the workers' wages. The workers who pay the piper cannot dictate even the note of the tune to be played. To facilitate this policy, 24 hours' notice has been introduced so that protestors may be got rid of at short notice.

The function of this group of imposed persons is to safeguard the employers against any demands of the men, and to protect the Owners against any individual or mass claims.

To cut a Price List is a simple matter in these circumstances. No consultation with the men; no mass meetings; the employers' desires operated through the nominal assent of their own hired thugs, paid for by compulsory deductions from the workers' wages. That is Fascism in Germany and Austria. How closely the position at Bedwas copies the German model, only you who are working there can appreciate.

In Germany, the Trade Union, the Welfare Clubs, the Workers' Athletic Grounds have been closed down by robbing them of the deductions for these concerns.

Bedwas follows the pattern. No deduction for the Workmen's Institutes, and no deduction for the Welfare Grounds.

Ignoring of Price Lists, failure to pay Compensation, payment to one Conveyor group out of the earnings of a different group, refusal to pay agreed rates for different grades of employment, pass without complaint. As in Germany, the complete abandonment of workers' rights is the normal condition of the Industrial Union's calling. The Workmen just have to "carry on," with no safeguard and no protection. Actually many of their rights are formally negotiated away by the heads of the so-called Union.

As in Germany, attendance at a Labour Meeting is a crime to be followed by a 24 hours' notice, and the actual spying on the Workmen for this purpose is carried out by the hirelings who are maintained by the deductions from the Workmen's wages.

At these Collieries all the elements of German Fascism are present, and in Bedwas in particular, Fascism is the instrument of the Company.

We call upon the men working at Bedwas and Taff Merthyr to repeat what has been done at Emlyn.

For eight years the Industrial Union fastened the men of Emlyn with the chains of "Scabbery." In two months they smashed these chains. The Miners' Federation will help you with all the resources at their disposal. We call upon you to band together in this fight. UNITY IS THE WAY TO VICTORY: SOLIDARITY IS YOUR PROTECTION: MASS ACTION WILL PREVENT VICTIMISATION. FORWARD TO TRADE UNION FREEDOM.

BEDWAS LODGE, S.W.M.F.

Oct., 1934 (N.S. No. 2.)

CYMRIC FEDERATION PRESS, NEVILLE STREET, CARDIFF.

One of the early leaflets issued by Ness Edwards to the Bedwas workforce.

25

SWMF Executive Council or the Bedwas Lodge. These leaflets exposed the true nature of the SWMIU and combined a focus on particular issues of concern to the workforce, with powerful statements about the broader issues at stake in Bedwas. One of Ness's common themes, echoing the views of Arthur Horner, was that the Industrial Union was nothing less than the "British form of Fascism". For Ness, the Company's Union's tactics contained "all the elements of the Hitler regime".

One of the first leaflets spelt out a "Charter for Bedwas". Eight demands were set out and these provided the focus of the campaign:

1. *The right to belong to the Miners' Federation.*
2. *The cancellation of the Pit Agreement which compels you to be members of a Company Union.*
3. *To establish freedom for normal trade union activities.*
4. *To give the workmen full control over their trade union contributions.*
5. *To give the workmen the right to appoint their own representatives without interference from the colliery Company.*
6. *To abolish intimidation of the workmen by the colliery management.*
7. *To establish the Federation Lodge to give the workmen adequate protection regarding compensation, wages, price lists and employment.*
8. *To abolish the twenty-four hour contract and replace it with a normal fourteen days' contract.*

There has been speculation that Ness "broke into" the Company's offices to obtain information about the SWMIU's collaboration with the colliery management. There is nothing to prove that this happened but Ness did acknowledge that a "Report Book", written by Industrial Union informers and kept in the colliery office, "fell into" the hands of the Federation. The information obtained was, again, given to the men at the pits in leaflet form.

In the vanguard of Ness's campaign were the victimised ex-Bedwas unemployed, organised in the Bedwas Unemployed Lodge. For the previous year or so, the main tasks of the Unemployed Lodge had been to give support to the unemployed and to run the large Workmen's Hall "as best they could", now that the colliery management had stopped all deductions from the men's pay. Under Ness's leadership the members of the Unemployed Lodge were now deployed at the colliery entrances to distribute daily leaflets and to obtain as much information as possible about what was happening in the colliery. As each shift left the colliery they were addressed by Federation officials. And in whatever communities the workforce was drawn from, personal contacts were made with individuals and small scale meetings were organised.

After a short time it was felt that real progress was being made and in June 1936, it was decided to take the campaign on to the next stage. The men at the colliery were asked to sign cards cancelling the authorisation of the Company to deduct

26

South Wales Miners' Federation.

OLIVER HARRIS,
GENERAL SECRETARY.

2, St. Andrew's Crescent,

Cardiff.

5th September. 1936.

To our fellow workmen down the Bedwas Pit.

The Executive Council considered today the document attached to this letter, and aftergiving it full consideration decided unanimously to accept these terms as a condition of withdrawing the notices calling a coalfield stoppage.

The Executive Council advises the workmen at Bedwas, and yourselves, that this stage having been reached the whole resources of the coalfield will be used to obtain the final success of complete recognition of the Federation at Bedwas.

We desire to congratulate you on your magnificent stand for freedom and sincerely trust that the decision of the Executive Council will be carried outwith all the faith and loyalty that have been so magnificently shown by you in the present incident.

You can be assured that the Executive Council will not let you down.

(signed)

The letter from the Federation which signalled the end of the dispute.

contributions for the SWMIU from their wages. Within a few days 200 men returned their cards, but the Company responded with threats of dismissal. In turn, the SWMF Executive made it clear that if a majority of the workforce signed cards revoking deductions, then the "whole force" of the SWMF would be used to stop victimisation.

Ness and his colleagues now worked even harder to increase the numbers opting-out of Industrial Union deductions. Buses were organised from places as far away as Dowlais and New Tredegar to bring men to a meeting at the Caerphilly Workmen's Hall. Over 300 attended and, in a highly charged meeting, the Company Union Report Book was displayed, allowing the men to see, for the first time, who had reported who. Ness also displayed a knuckleduster* which had been obtained from the Company's "armoury" and intended to be used against Federationists. Soon after this meeting, another meeting was held at the Bedwas Workmen's Hall, "in sight of the colliery and all its minions". The Bedwas meeting was attended by over 700 men and addressed by Arthur Horner and Ness Edwards.

Yet, despite his efforts, Ness candidly accepted that less than half of the workforce had switched allegiance to the Federation. Nevertheless, the SWMF Executive agreed to convene a coalfield conference with a recommendation that notices be tendered in support of the Bedwas men's right to join the Federation.

As the confrontation intensified, the Company showed no inclination to compromise. In fact, they stepped-up their efforts to identify and dismiss Federation sympathisers within the colliery after some of them had refused to become paid informers for the Company. The Company's position was spelt-out in a blunt and threatening letter given to every employee with their pay packet. Any miner who signed a form from the Federation which terminated their membership of the Industrial Union would be seen as wishing to "terminate his employment at the Colliery".

On 5 September the SWMF as a whole was due to withdraw its labour. However, just two days before, local miners' leaders met in secret in Abertridwr Workmen's Hall and agreed to deliberately pre-empt the situation by adopting the tactic of the 'stay down' strike, a tactic which had already been used to good effect in other collieries, particularly in nearby Nine Mile Point. The aim was for the night shift to stay underground in both Bedwas pits, and thereby bring the colliery to a halt. The initial response from the men was disappointing. But, although the numbers involved were not great, about 43 initially, the 'stay down' began to gather momentum and soon had an impact. News of the action spread quickly and similar 'stay downs' soon took place in a number of Rhondda collieries.

*This is almost certainly the same knuckleduster to be found amongst the Ness Edwards papers in the Coalfield Archive at Swansea University.

Under pressure from the Government, who feared that the situation could escalate further, the owners of the Bedwas Colliery informed the Government's Mines Department that they were prepared to meet with the SWMF. The Mines Department informed the Federation by telegram and immediately followed through with a series of telephone calls. It became clear that the Company was prepared to go much further than was initially thought, indicating that it was now willing to accept that:

1. *A ballot would be held at Bedwas to decide which union the men wanted*
2. *All propaganda at the pit would cease.*
3. *Notices to be withdrawn in the coalfield.*
4. *All Company Union officials not engaged at the colliery not to be allowed on the pit.*
5. *Discussions to start the following week.*

This information was now conveyed to the 'stay down' strikers at Bedwas, accompanied by a letter from the EC, warmly congratulating the men on their "magnificent stand for freedom". With some reluctance the strikers agreed to end their action and ascended the pit to a "tumultuous welcome" by the many thousands who had gathered. As Ness remarked, "The main part of the battle had been won, it was now up to the Federation officials to win the rest".

On the following day a mass meeting of the workforce was convened in the Bedwas Workmen's Hall and over 1,600 attended. The meeting began with the curtain being raised on the 43 stay down strikers who proceeded to sing their campaign song. Despite many serious doubts about the Executive's decision to call off the strike, the meeting, presided over by Bill Crews, nevertheless accepted what had been done.

Negotiations now proceeded with the Company during the following week, with Arthur Horner leading the SWMF negotiating team. However, on the first day the negotiations were abruptly stopped because of news of a fresh stay down strike at Bedwas. A rumour had spread in the colliery that the Company Union was planning a stay down strike itself, and so to prevent that, 173 men, supporting the Federation, took action. Arthur Horner responded swiftly, personally appealing to the men to call off their strike. His appeal worked and negotiations with the Company recommenced in London.

From the outset of the negotiations Horner made it very clear that his overriding concern was to secure recognition of the Federation as the one and only union in Bedwas. To secure this objective Horner was prepared to make concessions which many thought surprising, not least because he was a leading member of the Communist Party and had only recently been elected President of the SWMF on a radical platform. But Horner, as he later stated in his autobiography, knew that the

Company was in a parlous financial state. It followed that, "if there was a strike for a week or so at the colliery, the Company would be smashed. It would be the easiest thing in the world to close the Bedwas colliery for good. But we had no desire to destroy the men's employment at the cost of wiping out the Company Union, and so we set out to get the best possible agreement.

Even so, the 'moderation' of Horner surprised everyone, not least Samuel and Theodore Instone, the owners. Within a few weeks the negotiations were concluded on an agreement which was to stay in force for five years. In exchange for recognition of the Federation, Horner and his colleagues had agreed that there would be no restoration of the 1933 agreements, conditions and practices; instead, all the existing terms and conditions would continue; any employees who broke the agreement could be dismissed; the Federation would be unable to organise show cards or hold campaigns without the management's permission; the day-to-day contracts would continue for another year; there would be an independent and binding arbitration scheme; the basis of the men's representation would be a Committee made up of men employed at the colliery rather than the old lodge committee; and, significantly, the role of Miners' Agent would be carried out by Horner, as President of the Federation, and Saddler, as Vice-President. All of this was, of course, to be subject to a ballot of the workforce.

But before the recommendations were to be put to the miners at the colliery in a secret ballot, the Federation leadership had to win the support of the men at a mass meeting. Horner, Crews and Ness Edwards had the task of explaining the agreement at a meeting in the Bedwas Workmen's Hall. The meeting was difficult and very heated. For many of the Federationists present the proposed agreement gave far too much to the Company. Bedwas was being asked to accept arrangements which no other Federation-organised colliery had. They deeply resented the fact that strikes were being effectively banned, that many of the MIU customs and practices would be maintained, that 'blackleg' labour would be kept, and the members of the Fed who had lost their jobs through the Company's victimisation would still remain unemployed. It was also unacceptable to many activists that the Company was being given the authority to determine who would represent them at Lodge Committee level and even who would carry-out the role of Miners' Agent.

Horner, Crews and Ness Edwards did not have an easy ride. Horner, in particular, faced the brunt of much of the criticism. He gave the lead by attempting to put a positive gloss on the agreement. For example, he argued that there was "nothing in the agreement to stop a strike" and emphasised the differences between the current arrangements at the colliery under the MIU and what would happen under the Federation. The most difficult issue, though, was the rejection of Ness Edwards as Miners' Agent. Horner had attempted to justify this on the grounds that, as he had been the Chief Negotiator with the Company, the Company would hold him

The South Wales Miners' Industrial Union.

We pointed out on Monday that Mr. Ness Edwards stated from the platform of Bedwas Hall on Sunday that workmen at Bedwas sell their wives to keep their jobs. We have received the following letter from the wife of a Bedwas workman who has given us permission to print it :—

"To the men of Bedwas.—Are you going to defend your wife's honour? Are you going to allow Ness Edwards to take your wife's honour away? Are you going to stand by and have your fellow-workman looking at you and wondering if you are the blighter that has sold your wife for your job? Not only that, he has put every wife, mother and sister of every Bedwas workman under a stigma. If every one of them was of the same mind as me they would demand their husbands and sons to make him eat those words.

Fancy a man trying to win a fight through insulting remarks about women. It shows what methods they will take. Filthy minds and filthy ways. As a wife of a Bedwas workman I appeal to other wives and mothers to defend their honour. We have been free from all this trash for 4 years. Why tolerate such insults to enable the Federation to gain the day? **If you are loyal to your husband advise him to vote for the Miners' Industrial Union** and keep clean healthy minds and your jobs. There is no use in listening to all the promises of the Miners' Federation. **The Industrial Union has kept us in work for 4 years without any loud-speaking and shouting, only carrying out their work. I, for one, say " Carry on."**

This is from a Bedwas wife who intends to prove that she has not been sold so that her husband keeps his job."

(Signed) A BEDWAS WIFE.

A leaflet from the SWMIU attacking Ness Edwards.

31

responsible for the workforce's conduct if the Federation won the ballot. But it was Ness himself who won the day by making a "special appeal" to the meeting. Following his intervention the meeting accepted, unanimously, this point in the agreement.

Like Horner, Ness Edwards recognised that nothing was more important than securing the recognition of the SWMF at Bedwas. No doubt Ness found it embarrassing, possibly humiliating, to be excluded in this way and yet there is no inkling of this in anything Ness wrote or said. For him, the Fed came first.

The sensitivity of Ness's exclusion is underlined in the way this section of Clause 13 of the agreement was addressed in the Federation's main leaflet explaining the agreement to the men. After highlighting that "Mr. Ness Edwards has not had the sack", the leaflet went on to say:

> He will continue to work in the closest contact with the Bedwas workmen, and will be available for advice and service for the individual workman. We are satisfied that this is something that is temporary, and will probably settle itself when the "smoke of battle" has disappeared.

> In the operation and interpretation of the Agreement at Bedwas, the President and Vice-President will speak and act, not only as Miners' Agents but with the full weight of the Organisation behind them. This is not a bad thing for the Bedwas Workmen, for such power cannot fail in the legitimate efforts to improve and defend the conditions of the workmen.

The propaganda war between the SWMF and the MIU was now being conducted fervently by both sides; as the ballot date approached, so the intensity of the campaigns increased. The scab union focussed its attention mainly in two directions: firstly, it argued in its pamphlets and leaflets that Horner had negotiated a deal with the Company which either maintained or worsened the men's terms and conditions. The charge was that Horner and the Fed were only interested in securing recognition of the Federation and not winning improvements for the miners. The second theme which runs through much of the MIU's literature at this time is a series of personal references to Ness. The MIU had previously publicised the likelihood that Ness was to be excluded from the Agent's post before the final agreement had been reached. Now they attacked Horner, and sought to divide the Federation leadership, by condemning him for agreeing that the men would no longer be able to elect their Agent. Then, in a somewhat contradictory fashion, they condemned Ness as an unfit representative because of comments he is alleged to have made at a miners' meeting. According to the MIU, Ness had stated that workmen in Bedwas had "to sell their wives to keep their jobs". In the view of the Industrial Union:

no one but the foulest-mouthed hypocrite alive could say, as Mr. Edwards said, that workmen at Bedwas colliery sell their wives to keep their jobs. Only a being (not a man) with a mind like a sewer could imagine such a thing, leave alone make it the subject of a public statement.

In the same leaflet, among Ness's papers, held by Baroness Llin Golding, there is also another personal attack on Ness. Referring to Ness's earlier display of a scab union knuckleduster at a miners' meeting, the MIU criticised Ness for not explaining how he had obtained "this ironmongery" from an individual by the name of Billie Green. They then suggested that any "man" would not require "anything harder than a feather bolster to put Ness Edwards away".

In contrast to the MIU, the Federation in its literature did not attack individuals but highlighted the questionable financial links of the Industrial Union, its close relationship with management and, through close examination of its balance sheets, the relatively small amounts which were spent on furthering the interests of the miners. Little emphasis was placed on the fine detail of the proposed agreement.

The ballot was held under conditions which were scrupulously fair. Under the watchful eye of the Clerk to Monmouthshire County Council, 1,487 men cast their votes on 28 and 29 October 1936. There was a 91% turnout. The result was conclusive: 1,177 cast their votes for the Federation and a mere 309 for the Industrial Union. Ness acknowledged that to get the Bedwas men to accept the negotiated conditions had been "a real struggle". But the victory at Bedwas meant that "the last legitimate source of Company Union finance was stopped".

Bill Nind, the Communist secretary of the Bedwas Unemployed Lodge, wrote the following verse which was issued in leaflet form to the workforce after the result had been declared. Although Bill Nind was prevented from working again at Bedwas, the elation he felt at the overwhelming victory was very clear:

Bedwas Workmen's Farewell to M.I.U.

Poor OLD GREG* your time has come,
For barefaced cheek you take the bun.

From far and near you spread the cry,
That Bedwas men you'd satisfy.

But they were waiting for the day,
When they could openly have their say.

*William Gregory was the secretary of the SWMIU. He came from Heol-y-Cyw, near Bridgend.

That day has come and you must go,
Where trouble you will cause no more.

No longer will you meet the boss,
We've settled that matter with a cross.

We could have settled quick with dusters,
But Bedwas men are no mean rustlers.

We took the top of Arthur Horner,
To send you where it's very much warmer.

In Taff and Notts* you're "ON THE SPOT",
Try Chicago it's not so hot.

Al Capone will know you well,
For all you guys have a peculiar smell.

Tell Capone you have done your best,
But Bedwas men have sent you west.

SO LONG OLD PAL

W. J. Nind.
Shortfellow

With victory having been secured at Bedwas, the Federation again turned its attention to Taff-Merthyr. Following the 1934 stoppage, over 400 men at the colliery, plus 60 or so boys related to them or colliery officials, were still loyal to the MIU. It was now the aim of the Federation to win these over. Ness does not appear to have been involved in the final stages of the campaign. Instead, the EC relied on "old campaigners" who were drafted-in. To everyone's shock, following a negotiated settlement, not dissimilar to that in Bedwas, the Industrial Union won a secret ballot by 453 votes to 448.

The result, however, was somewhat academic. Within two weeks negotiations began for a 'merger' between the SWMF and the MIU, and in January 1938 agreement was reached on Terms to "wind-up" the SWMIU. Again, the terms were unacceptable to many of the lodge militants at Taff-Merthyr. The agreement, although coalfield-wide in its application, was also Taff-Merthyr specific and meant compromises being made by both sides. Ness strongly supported the agreement but he did accept that "Never in the history of the Federation had so much been paid for so little".

*The Nottingham coalfield was the heartland of the Spencer or Company Union.

34

Acceptance of the agreement was, nevertheless, necessary if the MIU was to be eradicated from the coalfield. The Federation EC gave its unanimous support to the agreement and, eventually, it received the backing of Federationists at Taff-Merthyr at a mass meeting in Bedlinog. Within two years Taff-Merthyr became a "normal Federation lodge" and Company unionism came to an end. Although criticised by many of the 'left' at the time, the tactics pursued by Arthur Horner proved to be effective. As Ness wrote in his unpublished history:

> *After twelve years of great struggle the coalfield was at last clean and the Federation could go forward ... to devote the whole of its attention to the service of the membership.*

However, this was not the end of the story. Uniquely, the Company Minutes of the meetings between the colliery management and the SWMF from December 1936 to January 1938 for the Bedwas colliery have survived. These handwritten Minutes cover a range of meetings which were held as a result of the October 1936 agreement. On the management side, depending on the meeting, amongst the attendees were the Colliery Agent, the Managers of the two pits at Bedwas and, on occasions, Sir Samuel Instone and Sir Theodore Instone. For the workforce were W. J. Saddler, Vice-President of the SWMF, Arthur Horner, President of the SWMF, (either or both acting as Agent), W. H. Crews (who was admitted after a number of months), and officers of the lodge. As well as the Minutes of the regular meetings between the two sides, there are also Minutes of the meetings which received deputations from the workforce, a meeting in London between Horner and Theodore Instone, and Minutes of an arbitration meeting in Cardiff.

What is recorded is extremely revealing. To begin with, it is quite clear that, despite the overwhelming vote in favour of the SWMF, for at least six months after the agreement was signed relations between the owners and management, and the majority of the workforce, remained strained. On numerous occasions the management claimed that the Federation was not adhering to the agreement. The Federation, in turn, alleged that the new workers being employed at the colliery were not joining the Federation, and that the management were "definitely assisting" former MIU members. The simmering unrest came to the fore on 9 March 1937. After months of friction between the manager at the North Pit, who was also the Chairman of the Trethomas Rent and Ratepayers' Association, and a number of men at the pit, 17 Federation men held a stay down strike in the North Pit. When approached by management at the pit floor soon after the strike had started, the men were abusive about Horner and shouted down "A. James [the Lodge Secretary] when he agreed with the [colliery] agent who reprimanded the men for breaking their agreement". The striking miners put forward 11 demands, top of the list being 100% Federation organisation. The second demand was that all local agreements be carried out.

Sir Samuel Instone responded with personal instructions that no discussions nor communications should take place with the men. He also suggested that the colliery agent should contact the police so that the men who had cut the underground signal telephone lines could be arrested for sabotage.

By the evening the men had recognised the futility of their action and, after watering-down their demands and having been visited by Saddler and Crews, they came to the surface. The men, who included amongst their number four members of the Lodge Committee, were then all dismissed. Despite repeated requests from the SWMF, the management steadfastly refused to re-instate them.

During the strike the management had accepted the "assistance" of Bill Crews and, following a meeting in London between Horner and the Instone brothers, it was agreed that Crews would be brought in to "deal with disputes". Although this was subsequently interpreted by the management to mean that he would be allowed to do this only on Thursdays, largely because of Bill Crews's efforts the situation in the colliery improved for the Federation over the next few months. His tact and experience proved very valuable, especially when the new Lodge Committee was so inexperienced and Horner had other commitments, including visiting Moscow on behalf of the Communist Party.

There was, however, no return for Ness Edwards. Even though the Federation had promised at the time of the ballot that his exile would be "temporary", the management was adamant that Ness would not have a role in the colliery. At a meeting in February 1937 the Colliery Agent stated that "We will never have anything to do with him". In another meeting Theodore Instone asked Horner if Ness Edwards was "treacherous", to which Horner replied, emphatically, that if Ness was "he would not be a member of the Miners' Federation".

Yet, there is no doubt that Ness continued to be held in the highest regard by the Federation men at Bedwas. The very fact that he was despised by the management and owners of Bedwas endeared him further to the men. It is significant, for example, that the third demand of the stay in strikers - only after full Federation membership and adherence to local agreements - was that Ness Edwards represent them at the colliery. Ness's standing was equally high across the coalfield as a whole. This was demonstrated by Ness's appointment by his colleagues on the SWMF EC to the Executive of the Miners' Federation of Great Britain in 1938.

Much of the above account of the Bedwas and Taff-Merthyr campaigns draws heavily on Ness's unpublished writings. Amongst Ness's papers is a near-final proof of four additional Chapters to Ness's first Volume of the *'History of the SWMF'*. These Chapters are entitled 'Company Union Attack', 'The Coal-field Awakes', 'Stay-down Miner', followed by a 'Conclusion'. Chronologically, the Chapters take us from the mid-1930s until the election of Arthur Horner as SWMF

President, just before the final phase of the campaign at Bedwas. The Chapters are type-set and the pages run from 162 to 229. Clearly, at the time of writing, it was intended by Ness that these four Chapters should form the concluding section of the first Volume. The question is why the Chapters were never included in the published book.

A possible explanation is that the four Chapters had been held back because they were to be the opening section of Ness's second Volume of the *'History of the SWMF'*. However, this is unlikely as at least two copies of the second Volume exist in typed draft, as well as there being hand-written notes for the Volume, and these have been written as if the four Chapters did not exist. The reasons for the Chapters' removal can only be connected with their 'sensitive content'.

Nearly 70 years after the Chapters were written it is perhaps difficult to appreciate just how controversial Ness's words were in the late 1930s. In the context of the extremely acrimonious industrial relations at Taff-Merthyr and Bedwas, Ness's words were politically explosive and potentially actionable. For instance, on page 172 in the first of the unpublished Chapters (which was to be Chapter XII of the first Volume), Ness refers to the policy of the management of Bedwas being "well indicated" by the "photograph of a document which came into our hands". This was to be reproduced in the book. The question is, of course, how did Ness obtain this and, indeed, other documents. Then, again, on page 203 there is a letter from Ness to the General Secretary of the SWMF. In it Ness strongly infers that there was a direct financial link between the management of Taff-Merthyr and the MIU. "Outside the Clerk's office on the colliery premises", wrote Ness, "Bevan, the Secretary of the Taff-Merthyr Branch of the Industrial Union, was standing talking to Milsom, the colliery cashier. We saw the cashier hand to Bevan a ledger-like book".

A second question is why the second Volume was never published. Perhaps the answer here is rather mundane. In comparison to the first Volume, even without its final Chapters, the second Volume, with only seven short Chapters, is quite brief. In an effort to avoid any suggestion of possible libel, it is not inconceivable that Ness 'toned down' the text to such an extent that the book became much attenuated and, therefore, less publishable. Alternatively, Ness's son, Alan, believes that his father did not want to publish because, in the charged atmosphere of the developing Cold War, Ness did not want to give any opportunity to the Communist Party to "glorify its past". Or it was simply the case that, when Ness became an MP and then a Government Minister, he had other things on his mind and never found the time to expand and complete the book.

Whatever the reason for its non-publication, the drafts of the second Volume make interesting reading. In terms of both the chronology and the material, there is an overlap between the second Volume and the unpublished Volume 1 Chapters. As suggested above, Ness chose to leave out a number of the more controversial and, therefore, interesting episodes in his second Volume draft. For example, there is not even a passing reference to the 'riot' in Bedwas in March 1933, even though its significance cannot be underestimated.

The six Chapters of the typed draft of the second Volume take us from an overview of the coalfield after the First World War to the end of the struggle against Company Unionism. The draft ends with a concluding Chapter which focuses on some of the "big men" of the Federation, who, Ness tells us, "in any day or generation ... would have been outstanding characters".

'Mabon', William Abraham, heads the list, followed by Brace, Winstone, Hartshorn, Morrell, Arthur Jenkins, James Griffiths and Arthur Horner. The warmest tribute is, however, saved for Tom Richards. From the formation of the Fed in 1898 until November 1931, Richards had been its General Secretary. During that long period of office, Ness explained that Richards's success lay in the fact that he was "Cautious and shrewd, never in a hurry, he had all the characteristics of the craftsman collier". Ness believed that Tom Richards "had no great platform ability, but in a negotiating room he was the biggest man in the room". Although Richards was hardly a radical, he was in temperament and politics a Lib-Lab of the "old school", he had one outstanding quality which impressed Ness above all others - he always put the interests of the Federation first. As Ness put it "To him the Federation was sacred, and was to be preserved at all costs. Without it the miners would be lost, and this love of the machine for the protection of the miner was one of his outstanding characteristics". Ness's praise for Tom Richards is fascinating, not least because it says as much about Ness and his absolute loyalty to the Fed as it does about Tom Richards.

Just as Ness was elected to the Executive of the MFGB in 1938, the dark cloud of fascism was rapidly descending upon Europe. By the end of that year Nazi Germany had occupied the Sudetenland and there was a real concern that the miners' leaders who had fled to other parts of Czechoslovakia would be sent back to face certain death.

On 16 February 1939 the MFGB Executive responded by deputing Ness Edwards to travel immediately to Prague to make contact with miner refugees and arrange for their evacuation. This Ness did and returned to South Wales with around 100 refugees. Initially it seems that the refugees went to Virginia Park in Caerphilly, before going to the Ship Hotel in Penarth. The hotel was vacant at the time and the owners, Brains Brewers Limited of Cardiff, made it available free of charge. All the other costs, including the renovation needed at the hotel and the cost of supporting the refugees for six months, was met by the SWMF, after an appeal to the Districts in the Federation.

38

On the eve of the Second World War, Ness Edwards was widely recognised as one of the most effective leaders of the South Wales Miners' Federation. He had organised extremely successful campaigns against Company Unionism in Taff-Merthyr and Bedwas and had probably done more than anyone else to ensure that the Fed was, once more, the one and only voice of miners in South Wales. He had also won recognition on the national stage and had demonstrated his internationalism in the most practical of ways. There can be little doubt that in early 1939 Ness saw his life continuing to revolve around the Federation and the coal industry. The unexpected death of the Labour MP for Caerphilly was to turn Ness's life upside down.

Ness as a young man,
probably in his Sunday best.

The young Ness when he was a
student in the central Labour College.

Six Bells Colliery in Abertillery where Ness first found employment.

Penallta Colliery in the Rhymney Valley where Ness was appointed Lodge Secretary in 1927.

The Bedwas Colliery which was at the centre of the struggle against company unionism.

Police escorting a 'Blackleg' past the central buildings in Trethomas.

The police on 'Blackleg' duty in Navigation Street, near the entrance to the Bedwas Colliery.

A solitary 'Blackleg' is accompanied on his way home, walking past the Ty-Yn-Y-Pwll (Pike) Public House in Trethomas.

The 'stay down' strikers are given a heroes' welcome outside the Bedwas Workmen's Hall

A Bedwas 'stay down' striker is welcomed by his wife holding their child in a traditional Welsh shawl.

Arthur Horner, Ness Edwards and W. H. Crews (from left to right) near the Fed. Offices in Cardiff.

CHAPTER 3

LABOUR MP AND GOVERNMENT MINISTER

There is nothing to suggest that Ness had considered becoming a Member of Parliament before 1939. In May of that year, the Labour MP for Caerphilly, Morgan Jones, died suddenly at the age of 53. He had apparently contracted a mysterious illness in the Caribbean a month earlier, after having visited the West Indies as a Member of the Royal Commission investigating conditions on the islands.

Morgan Jones, like Ness, had been a conscientious objector during the First World War, playing a leading role nationally in the anti-war movement. Both men had been active members of the ILP. But Morgan Jones's background was, in many ways, quite different from that of Ness. Born in Gelligaer above the Rhymney Valley, Morgan Jones was a university-educated school teacher who made widening educational opportunities his life long crusade. He also had a wide experience of local government, having served on Glamorgan County Council and its Education Committee for many years. Quite naturally then, Morgan Jones's affinity within the Divisional Labour Party in Caerphilly tended to be with the local councillors and Ward members rather than with the local leadership of the SWMF. It is hardly surprising that, when the highly respected MP died, the local press and indeed many Labour Party members thought it unlikely that a miners' nominee would win the Labour nomination. This view was compounded by the fact that the Federation could already boast 12 members among Wales's 18 Labour MPs, and some saw this as already too many.

In the selection process, Ness was put forward as the miners' nominee, after the miners decided that there would be only a single miners' nomination, and he received 26 out of a total of 60 nominations. In the view of the *Merthyr Express* this meant that "the great bulk of Labour in the division do not approve of the suggestion that Caerphilly should be represented by a miner". The outcome of the selection conference proved the newspaper wholly wrong. Five candidates were shortlisted: they were Mr. W. J. Jenkins of Pembroke, Cllr. Tom Evans (Chairman of Glamorgan County Council Finance Committee), Mr. W. Davies of Trecenydd, Caerphilly, Mr. Frank James, Cardiff (Organiser for the Transport and General Workers' Union) and Ness Edwards. Then, on 10 June in Ystrad Mynach they appeared before 171 delegates representing Ward Parties and affiliated organisations. Each spoke for five minutes and answered two questions. Ness received 94 votes on the first ballot and, with an overall majority, was duly selected as the Labour candidate.

The by-election which followed was a low-key formality. All sections of the local Labour Party rallied quickly behind their candidate and were urged to "secure support" for Ness on the basis of his experience and background as a miners' leader. Ness's rallying cry to the electors was to "Remain True".

In his election address Ness stressed both international and domestic issues. He called for a common Peace Front of Britain, France and Russia to resist "Fascist aggression" in line with the principles of the League of Nations' Covenant. This, Ness believed, was "the only road to peace".

On the domestic agenda Ness focussed on the continuing levels of high unemployment, the plight of "old-age pensioners", who were "condemned to end their days in hunger and want", and the need to bring about "health and happiness for the people". He said Labour's goal was to achieve real prosperity based on:

> *public ownership and control of Finance, Land, Transport, Coal and Power. Only by this means can the wealth of the Nation be utilised for the full benefit of the Nation.*

Ness then went on to explain that:

> *The well-being and happiness of the people are Labour's first concern. The Social Services must be maintained and improved. The purchasing power of the people must be raised. Work or adequate maintenance must be found for the unemployed. The Family Means Test must be abolished.*

In uncompromising tone Ness's address continued:

> *Better wages, shorter hours, Holidays with Pay as a legal right, a plentiful supply of good food at reasonable prices, the raising of the school leaving age, with maintenance allowances; adequate rates of compensation for the victims of industry; Workmen's Compensation Act reform; new Mining Safety Legislation; all these urgently needed reforms are part of Labour's Programme.*

Ness then made an appeal for nothing less than a "New Social Order" and support for building a "Better Britain", before concluding with the following:

> *Let the people of this Constituency at this By-Election give a lead to the Nation.*
> *Let Caerphilly remain true.*

41

The voters of the Caerphilly Division responded well and although there was a slightly reduced turn-out (not uncommon in by-elections), on 4 July 1939 Ness secured a very comfortable victory. The result was:

Electors	Turnout	Candidate	Votes	Labour Majority
42,678	68.4%	N. Edwards (Lab)	19,847	10,498
		R.M. Bell (Con)	9,349	

The miners, as recorded in the Penallta Lodge Minutes, played an active part in the campaign and there was understandable satisfaction amongst them that their Agent had won such an emphatic result. In those same Lodge Minutes there is a wonderful tribute recorded to Ness by his close friend Bill Crews on behalf of the members of the Federation in the area. Bill Crews stated that the miners of the area were "proud of the fact" that Ness Edwards had been elected as their MP. "He is", wrote Bill Crews, "a young man who has had a good training in every phase of working class life". Looking back over the time Ness had been in the Rhymney Valley, Bill Crews specifically referred to the struggles against the Company Union at Taff-Merthyr and Bedwas as "incidents … that will become historically 'High Spots'". He also acknowledged Ness's less high profile but equally important work on behalf of silicosis victims and the unemployed. Bill Crews concluded by expressing the hope that Ness would "live long to render service to the people who saw fit to elect him as their Representative to the House of Commons".

As a new MP Ness was not in any way overawed by the Palace of Westminster. Taking forward his electoral promises, Ness immediately took up the issues which concerned the people he represented and his maiden speech to the House of Commons was a clear indication of the kind of issues on which he was to focus his attention. 'Catching the Speaker's Eye' in a debate on a Motion of Censure on the Government's policy towards pensioners, Ness spoke with passion about the plight of elderly people he knew personally: in one part of his speech Ness referred to the many elderly people who had no option but to work, while younger men were unemployed:

> *There lives not far from my home in South Wales a collier, who, at the age of 71, is still working. He has given nearly 60 years of his life to the mines. He has produced an untold quantity of wealth for the State. He has helped to make millionaires with his labour, and there he is, at a time when he should be able to take a well-earned rest, struggling to keep going, because this Government know no gratitude towards those who have made the largest contribution to the wealth and well-being of the State. I am satisfied that in the mining industry the large majority of aged miners would be only too glad to take a rest in the winter of their days if only the pension were adequate to maintain themselves without having to*

be beholden to private charity or parish relief. Nearly 400,000 are in this position, and it ought not to be beyond the wit of this Government to give the old ones a rest and the young ones a change to live their own lives in decent wage-earning employment.

He went on to quote another example:

I know the home of a collier intimately. He started work in the mines at the age of 10 and worked up to 1924, when the depression hit South Wales. He had brought up a family of seven children on the standard of decency common to our mining villages. He had got together a respectable home. He had scraped to buy his own cottage. In the long lean years since he became unemployed he has used up all his resources. His rates went unpaid, until the outstanding debts were greater than the available assets. The cottage was sold to meet the debts. I have been in the habit of visiting that household on each birthday of this unemployed collier. Last year I again visited it on his birthday. It was his sixty-fifth. This birthday was not a day of celebration and congratulations. The miserable bit of unemployment assistance, some 27s. per week, had come to an end. Henceforward, because the wife was some years younger, the total income was to be 10s. That birthday was a day of tragedy. Independence was gone. Pride had to be swallowed, and he and his wife had to ask their sons and daughters to keep them until the day when the grave claimed them. When Hon. Members opposite talk of other resources which our people are supposed to have, I cannot forget the tears in the eyes of my own mother on the day that my father reached his sixty-fifth birthday.

After dismissing the arguments of the Tories who claimed "that the country cannot afford to keep its aged people", Ness concluded his speech with an effective turn of phrase:

Here is a great human problem, and this House is asked to deal with it in such a way as to warrant not only calling itself the Mother of Parliaments, but also the mother of its own people.

Typically, Ness's speech was well researched and eloquently delivered. It combined local examples of individual hardship with wider descriptions of poverty. The scene was now well and truly set for Ness's Parliamentary career which was to unfold over the next 30 years. It was to be a career which was characterised with passionate, yet well informed oratory and principle combined with practicality.

43

PARLIAMENTARY DIVISION OF CAERPHILLY
GENERAL ELECTION - 1945
POLLING DAY, THURSDAY, JULY 5th - - 8 a.m. to 9 p.m.

Daily Herald photo

VOTE FOR
NESS EDWARDS
THE LABOUR CANDIDATE

No matter what your Politics, please read this Election Address

Ness's election address for the 1945 general Election.

During his first few years as an MP, Ness concentrated on mastering the nuances of Parliamentary procedure and contributing to debates on subjects about which he was well informed. He was prominent, for example, in the debates on the introduction of Bevin boys in the collieries and the call-up of miners. In these debates Ness was not afraid to speak his mind and in February 1941 he joined Aneurin Bevan and eight other Welsh Labour MPs in breaking the Party Whip by putting forward an amendment to the National Government's 'Determination of Needs Bill'. The issue was 'public assistance' for the unemployed and Ness wanted nothing less than the abolition of the hated means test, not just its removal from households. Predictably, the amendment was lost but such was the annoyance of the Party leadership with the rebellion that, it has been suggested, Clem Attlee told Ness that he would personally make sure that he would never have a job in a future Labour Government.

Ness's interest in the coal mining industry led him to become Secretary of the Miners' Group of MPs in 1942 and throughout his years in Parliament he never failed to champion the miners' cause. In 1945, in recognition of his efforts in evacuating miners' families before the war, Ness was asked by the Miners' Federation to represent the British miners at the memorial to those murdered by the Nazis at Lidice in Czechoslovakia. Ness's association with Czechoslovakia continued and for many years he remained a Patron of the British-Czechoslovak Friendship League.

However, the most traumatic visit Ness made in 1945 was to the Buchenwald concentration camp in Germany. In the spring of 1945, as stories about the Nazi concentration camps began to seep out, there was an understandable disbelief at the scale of the horror which was being revealed. Even in the corridors of the House of Commons some Members thought that newspaper reports were exaggerated "atrocity-mongering". So, to provide undeniable evidence of what had happened, Ness approached the Joint Chief Whip, who then met Winston Churchill, the Prime Minster, to discuss what should be done. Churchill responded by making an announcement in the House of Commons stating that he had received an informal message from General Eisenhower saying that the discoveries at Buchenwald were far worse than anything previously seen. Churchill explained that he had been invited to send a group of MPs who would be able to see for themselves the atrocities and, thereby, provide proof of what had happened. On the following morning, Ness and nine other volunteer MPs flew out to Germany.

What Ness and his colleagues saw at Buchenwald was truly appalling. As they were driven from Weimar Airport towards Buchenwald they met hundreds of slave labourers dressed in pyjama-like suits, drudging west, away from the camp. Then, as they came closer to Buchenwald a terrible smell wafted towards them. The stench was so strong that Ness momentarily fainted.

Buchenwald was a slave camp for 120,000. According to the documents left behind by the Nazis, over 51,000 had died, 17,000 of those between January and April 1945. Thousands more had been marched away from the camp the day before the Americans had arrived. Although the camp had been liberated a week earlier, it was still a scene of indescribable filth, horror and human degradation.

At the camp gate the group was soon surrounded by hundreds of emaciated men, all wanting to know how soon it would be before they would be able to go back to their homes. As the group entered the camp they saw on their right a brick building with a high chimney. This, they learned, was the incinerator, in front of which was a huge pile of naked, decomposing dead bodies ready to be burned. On the parade ground was a four rope gibbet and opposite the entrance to the inner compound they saw a whipping chair. A little further away was a large pile of human ashes, awaiting local farmers to collect them for use as fertilizer. Everywhere was the overwhelming stench of human decay and dozens upon dozens of skeleton-like figures aimlessly shuffling around.

In an article for the *Western Mail*, some 16 years later, at the start of the trial of Adolf Eichmann for crimes against humanity, Ness described what he and his colleagues had witnessed as they went around the camp:

> *First we went to the basement of the incinerator building. A row of meat hooks were set into the wall on which the bodies had been hung by the throat to await the readiness of the furnaces.*

> *At the back of the building, at ground level, was a trap-door covering a shaft to the basement. The intended victims would be made to walk on to the trap-door and as they fell they were clubbed to death at the bottom then hung on the hooks on the way to the furnaces. This was the end of the road for the useless, including the slave girls who had been used as prostitutes, as they lost their charms or became pregnant.*

> *Hut 61 was regarded as the hospital hut. The only difference, however, was the rough table at the end on which the German and slave doctors did their operations without anaesthetics.*

> *Here the shelves were full of bodies, some dead and the rest doomed to die. The human excreta dripped from shelf to shelf, those below being unable to move away. Typhus lice were everywhere, and soon we too harboured many in our clothes.*

The memories of Buchenwald were to stay with Ness for the rest of his life. As well as those distressing recollections, Ness also left the concentration camp with a lampshade made from human skin which had probably been taken off someone when they were still alive. This was not a macabre souvenir but a graphic, physical reminder of man's inhumanity to man. Today, the lampshade is in St. Martin's Comprehensive School in Caerphilly.

In December 1989 Llin Golding, Ness's daughter and then the MP for Newcastle-under-Lyne, made a moving speech in the Commons in favour of the controversial War Crimes Bill, the purpose of which was to allow the prosecution of alleged war criminals living in Britain. Recalling what her father had told her and her brothers and sisters on his return from Buchenwald, Llin explained how traumatic Ness's visit had been for him. When he returned to Britain Ness had great difficulty sleeping and continued having nightmares for "very many years". In 1995 Peter Hill, the BBC Parliamentary Correspondent, described her speech as "Possibly the most harrowing speech heard in the Commons" since the House was first broadcast. The speech is included in a compilation of recordings made by the BBC and EMI of 'Great Parliamentary Speeches' 1978-1994.

In the General Election of July 1945 Ness proclaimed in his 'Election Special' that the choice for the people was clear: "Shall it be a future controlled by the monopolistic big-business gang behind Churchill, or shall it be controlled by representatives of the people for the people?" Following an enthusiastic Labour campaign, culminating in a huge open-air rally at The Twyn, in the centre of Caerphilly, the result for Ness was overwhelming. Ness trounced his Conservative opponent by securing over 80% of the vote. Across the country as a whole, Labour had a landslide victory.

With the election of a Labour Government, Ness's hard work on the backbenches, and the experience he had gained as a trade union official, were recognised when he was appointed to the Government as Secretary to the Ministry of Labour and National Service. Although a Junior Minister, Ness was to play a crucial role, alongside two other former Welsh miners' leaders, Nye Bevan and Jim Griffiths, in helping to lay the foundations for the new Britain that Labour was determined to build.

Under the Minister, George Isaacs, and with the assistance of the young MP George Brown, who was Ness's Parliamentary Private Secretary, Ness had responsibility for selecting those displaced foreign workers who would be able to settle in Britain and contribute to rebuilding the country's economy. With Isaacs determining the principles which were to be followed, it was Ness who had the task of putting them into practise. Over 95,000 displaced or homeless refugees were brought to Britain under schemes for European voluntary workers, along with about 100,000 Poles and 15,000 German ex-prisoners of war. Many of these workers came to South Wales; all were grateful for the opportunity to create a new life.

Ness also had the crucial task of guiding demobilised members of the armed forces back to industry with the maximum speed and the minimum of disruption. The priorities were to ensure there were sufficient men in the building industry: to raise the skills levels of the men and women who had been demobilised, and to train the unemployed for the most urgent social tasks. The most difficult issue which Ness had to face was the mismatch between the demands of industry for a speedy demobilisation and the continuing needs of the armed forces. This meant that a number of skilled workers who had previously worked in reserved occupations had to be called-up. This was a difficult problem but Ness handled it with enormous skill and diplomacy. Some thought the measures the Government was now introducing were unnecessary, but Ness said to those who asked the question who are we defending our country against, "We are defending our country against anyone who would attack us". Making use of his negotiating skills, Ness gained the support and co-operation of the trade unions for his radical plans.

A particularly testing moment for Ness was the unofficial London Dockers' strike, which led the Government to declare a state of emergency. Suspecting the influence of Communist militants, Ness declared that the loyalty of the dockers should be to their "fellow workers in Britain" rather than to Communists in the Soviet Union. Ness's support for the Government's tough line, however, brought stinging criticism from S. O. Davies, the MP for Merthyr and a fellow miners' MP. In the House of Commons, 'S.O.' declared that "the invoking of these powers is a disaster", and then, in a barbed reference to their shared past, 'S.O.' went on to state that "judging from the happy smile on his face since I got up, the Rt. Hon. Member for Caerphilly seems pleased to have forgotten our experiences in South Wales".

Such criticism undoubtedly hurt Ness but he was adamant that the election of a Labour Government, facing difficult challenges, required "responsibility" from the trade union movement. It was Ness's firm belief that the Government was "on the right road to a solution between the totalitarianism method and the method of unrestricted private enterprise", and ill-discipline and narrow self-interest should not be allowed to threaten this.

As a Junior Minister with a difficult portfolio, Ness won plaudits from all sides, even the Conservative opposition. Indeed, the relatively calm state of industrial relations after 1945, in marked contrast to the period after the First World War, was in large part due to the skill and effort of Ness Edwards.

Such was Ness's success in his first ministerial office, in 1947 he was included in the King's Birthday Honours and made a Privy Counsellor. In both London and South Wales, his 'elevation' was warmly welcomed. Amongst Ness's personal papers is an impressive collection of letters from constituents and well-wishers across the country, all bestowing fulsome praise and congratulations on Ness.

One of the most interesting letters is one from a non-Labour supporting constituent. Although he declared himself of different political leanings to Ness,

10, Downing Street,
Whitehall.

19th September, 1951.

My dear Ness

I have decided to proceed to a General Election in October and an announcement will be made at 9 p.m. to-night. Meanwhile I would ask you to keep the information strictly to yourself.

I should have liked to have called all Ministers together, but this would inevitably have caused the Press to draw the inference and to anticipate the announcement.

You may be sure that I have taken advice on this matter and have weighed carefully the pros and cons before deciding.

I need not detail the conflicting considerations which no doubt will occur to you.

I shall have a meeting of Ministers next week.

Yours sincerely,

C.

The Right Hon. Ness Edwards, M.P.

The letter from the Prime Minister which effectively meant the end of Ness's Ministerial career.

he nevertheless explained that he wanted to offer his congratulations as he felt that if he had "a just cause" and required the assistance of his MP, then he knew Ness would pursue it with "vigour and persistence". This letter is worth quoting, not merely because it is indicative of the widespread pleasure at Ness's honour, but because it reflects the hard work which Ness was doing at a local level as a "Constituency MP". It is all too easy to devalue or underestimate the ongoing commitment of an MP like Ness to the people he represented, especially when he held Ministerial responsibility. Amongst the older generation in the Caerphilly constituency many people still 'sing the praises' of Ness for his consistent work on behalf of his constituents.

Ness also had plenty of, what today we would call, "hinterland". He always recognised there was more to life than politics. His family, who Ness 'protected' from the harsh world of politics, was always supremely important to him; he enjoyed 'pottering' in his garden, had a love of literature and music and had a real enthusiasm for rugby. In 1950 Ness and his son, Rhys, were instrumental in helping to establish the Caerphilly Harlequins, the forerunner of Caerphilly RFC, and Ness became the Club's first President a position he held until his death.

Despite his heavy workload at this time, Ness found time to write a short pamphlet on *'Caerphilly and its Castles'*. The pamphlet draws together information from all the secondary sources available at the time and is a very readable introduction to Caerphilly's magnificent medieval castle which was rebuilt by the Marquis of Bute. Sadly, however, hardly any of Ness's pamphlets remain. Shortly after the pamphlet was published it was pointed out to Ness that a relatively minor error had been made in the text on page 11 Prince Edward, the son of Henry III, is incorrectly referred to as The Black Prince. Apparently, Ness was so incensed by his mistake that he tried to burn all the copies of the pamphlet in a large bonfire at the bottom of his garden. The only copy the author has seen is a singed copy which was rescued from the fire by his daughter, Llin.

The 1950 General Election did not go well for Labour. The Party won but now had only a small majority. For Ness the election campaign was dominated by one somewhat unusual issue the Tonypandy Riots of 1910. The events of 1910 in Tonypandy had helped to form the consciousness of the South Wales coalfield and Winston Churchill had become reviled because of his role in those disturbances. So, when Churchill made a speech in Cardiff during the 1950 election campaign in which he told, what he called, "the true story of Tonypandy" and claimed that when he was Liberal Home Secretary he had not sent troops against the miners of the Rhondda, there was widespread indignation and anger across South Wales. Churchill alleged that he had stopped the movement of troops to the area and, instead, had sent 150 Metropolitan Police with the sole object of preventing loss of life. The only contact with the rioters, claimed Churchill, was by unarmed London Police who charged with "rolled-up mackintoshes".

Ness responde'd with passion and hard facts. He said Churchill's claims were "a cruel lie", a "masquerade of the truth", a statement "deplorable in a statesman of such eminence". By referring to the autobiography of General Macready, the Commanding Officer of the soldiers, as well as contemporary newspaper reports, Ness was able to demonstrate what had actually happened.

Ness explained that on 9 November 1910 one squadron of Hussars had arrived at Pontypridd and on the following day were sent to guard the colliery offices in the Rhondda. In addition, Ness quoted the *Western Mail*, traditionally the newspaper of the coal owners, as reporting that "a detachment of the North Lancashire Regiment and the Lancashire Fusiliers were despatched from Swindon to Pontypridd. The newspaper also reported on 10 November that Churchill, as Home Secretary, had sent an order to Pembroke Arsenal to prepare "several thousand rounds of ball ammunition for use by the troops against the strikers in South Wales", and that 150 Cavalry had arrived at Aberdare together with ambulance men from Cardiff.

Ness pointed out that in Macready's autobiography it was stated that there were two squadrons of Cavalry deployed at Pontypridd, Infantry Companies at Llwynypia in the Rhondda and in Aberaman in the Cynon Valley, and two Reserve Companies at Newport. In order to counter the tactics of the striking miners, Macready wrote:

> *... small bodies of Infantry on the high ground, keeping level with the police on the main road, moved slowly down the side track and by a little gentle persuasion with the bayonet drove the stone-throwers into the arms of the police on the lower road.*

For Ness, these were the facts "recorded not by a romantic politician but by the Tory newspaper at the time and the Commanding Officer of the forces deployed. Mr. Churchill *did* use the military against the miners at Tonypandy, and the miners will never forget it". Ness emphatically stated that "for Churchill to say the police only used their rolled-up capes is a deliberate lie. They made many attacks on men with their batons". And if Macready's autobiography and newspaper reports were insufficient evidence, Ness declared that he himself had actually seen the soldiers in action.

Given the undeniable success which Ness had made of his first ministerial post, it was of little surprise that when Clem Attlee, the Prime Minister, announced his new Government after the 1950 General Election, Ness was promoted. The position he was given was that of Postmaster General. If Ness's promotion was no surprise, it was a disappointment to Ness that he was not given a seat in the Cabinet. When Ness reported on his promotion to his Constituency Labour Party, while he expressed his obvious pleasure about his new appointment, he nevertheless made known his disappointment about not being made a member of the Cabinet. Apparently, when Ness indicated his disappointment to Attlee, the Prime Minister reminded him that he himself had at one time been Postmaster General.

With responsibility for the Post Office, including telecommunications, Ness now presided over, what he called, "a massive industry, a huge social service". As the Post Office then employed more than 354,000 people, handled 8,000 million letters per annum, and nearly 250 million parcels, and had a growing savings bank and an expanding telephone network, Ness was entirely correct in describing the Post Office as a "great department" which touched "every single member of the community and renders a service to every member of the community".

Ness was enormously proud of the Post Office and was, by all accounts, a popular Postmaster General with both staff and public alike. A glance at the monthly *Post Office Magazine* for the short time Ness was Postmaster General indicates how active he was. Every week meant visits to Post Offices, telephone exchanges, presentations and social events in all parts of the country. Tony Benn, himself a future Postmaster General, recognised Ness's hard work in the position and acknowledged that Ness sought to introduce into the Post Office the principles of "guild socialism". In December 1950 Ness made the traditional BBC radio broadcast on the Home Service, urging customers to "Post early for Christmas". The recording of his broadcast is truly fascinating. Ness's message is delivered in a way typical of the BBC at the time; his words are precise, clear and almost school-masterly in tone. There is a slightly gruff edge to Ness's voice, no doubt assisted by regular smoking and, despite the effort to minimise any trace of a Welsh Valley's accent, at the end of most sentences there are typically Welsh melodic cadences.

Ness was adamant that to expand and meet the growing demand for services, the Post Office needed one thing above all else - extra resources. One of the first things that Ness had to do on his appointment was to steer through Parliament a Bill to enable the Post Office to undertake £75 million of capital development.

Most of the money for which Ness was asking Parliament was intended for the Post Office. However, the Post Office, as an organisation, was responsible for providing the links between television transmitting stations and some of the money Ness requested was to extend these links. Television was *the* new development of the age and Ness used the opportunity of the Second Reading of the Bill, and his Maiden Speech as Postmaster General, to announce that "in a little more than two years' time television should be made available to about 70% of the population of Britain". This was indeed Britain keeping "abreast of the world".

Although not as sure-footed in his new role as many expected, Ness succeeded in steering through his first piece of legislation. He then went on to introduce unpopular, though necessary measures to raise postal charges and found imaginative ways to increase the Post Office's income, such as reintroducing the greetings telegram.

Ness also introduced the first ever Telephone Bill in Parliament. This was to allow the telephone service to be run on a more effective and "business-like" basis. And, again using his trade union experience, Ness sought to bring about a more rational system of industrial relations in the postal industry. Speaking at a conference of the Union of Post Office Workers, Ness reiterated a message he had made before: "We have great power; we have entered the doors of the House, but far too many still knock on the door forgetting we have occupied the House". By this Ness meant that "in the society through which we are moving today we require from the trade union movement the highest degree of statesmanship".

Nor was this enough. In the Post Office there were no fewer than 35 trade unions. Ness recognised that such a situation had the potential of creating chaotic industrial relations, particularly when there was aggressive inter-union rivalry. In the House of Commons in July 1950, Ness expressed his frustration by referring to a situation where an impasse had been created because unions were blaming each other for a particular problem. There was, he said, "political support" for "a spirit of indiscipline, in some cases a spirit of sabotage ... a spirit of non-cooperation and a vendetta between various members of staff". The "political" interference to which he referred was supposedly from the Conservative Party. Although these words were unscripted and Ness spoke in reply to a debate, they caused an outcry during the summer of 1950 from some of the trade unions. Such was the furore that, when Ness next came to the Despatch Box, he felt obliged to make a tactical retreat. First, he admitted that he had not made the best choice of words and then he made it clear that he had not intended any "general condemnation" of the staff of the Post Office. Finally, Ness claimed that the examples of industrial unrest to which he referred were "hypothetical".

Despite the difficulty which Ness found himself in, there is no doubt that industrial relations in the Post Office was a huge problem. Although Ness clearly allowed himself to be carried away, he had the courage to address these problems 'head on' and, in so doing, encouraged the unions themselves to begin a process of dialogue which was to lead to future rationalisation.

It was, however, the issue of 'finance' which dominated Ness's time as Postmaster General. Soon after he was appointed, Ness formed the view that the Post Office was suffering from a "Gladstonian idea of finance". By which he meant that the Post Office was harnessed, against its best interests, to the priorities of the Treasury.

Ness believed that while it was perfectly in order for the Post Office "to make some contribution to the Exchequer" it should not be regarded "as an instrument of fiscal policy or a means of taxing the community". Ness's vision of the Post Office was of an organisation "free from all strings which are imposed upon it" because of "its relationship to the Treasury". This was a huge struggle to win and although Ness made some progress in freeing controls on the developing telephone service, it was a number of years before the Post Office achieved anything approaching the business autonomy which Ness had wanted. But, again, Ness should be credited for taking the first, crucial steps by developing ideas which were clearly ahead of their time. In the Post Office and elsewhere in British industry Ness believed it was vital to have new attitudes and fresh thinking, but he thought it necessary to first "rear a new generation of technicians imbued with the right outlook based on the proper philosophy".

Ness's justified pride in the Government of which he was part was well articulated in his reply to the Welsh Affairs debate in the House in December 1950. "It will be remembered", he told Members, that "before the war, Wales was dying of pernicious economic anaemia. Our people were drifting away; there was poverty [in our lands]; housing was going to the dogs. ... houses in my own constituency were sold for £20. That was the state of affairs in South Wales, and, indeed, in one part of Senghenydd there was a row of houses which no one would buy because the colliery there had been bought and shut down bought in London one day and shut down the next and the whole community was dislocated".

Now things were very different; everyone had seen an improvement in their standard of living:

> *I would ask the miners: which they would rather have - what they knew between the two World Wars, when their average wage was £2.6s.5d with all the talk of victimisation, fighting the scab unions, the hooter blowing for a stopped day or the guaranteed week with an average wage of £8.3s.0d and holidays with pay today?*

> *One could talk about the farmer and the farmworker and the young women who now have a chance to find a job in Wales instead of trekking to London to work in cheap domestic service. The only industry in Wales which is not thriving today is the pawn-broking industry. Wales has something to sing about in the progress now being made.*

Ness's work as Postmaster General came to an abrupt end when Labour lost the 1951 General Election. In Caerphilly, Ness held the seat comfortably with a majority of well over 22,000. But this was small comfort when Labour lost power nationally, even though its percentage of the vote actually increased. Ness braced himself for opposition and agreed to continue to serve on Labour's Frontbench. Little did Ness, or any other Labour MP, realise that Labour was to remain in opposition for 13 long years.

CHAPTER 4

FIGHTING IN THE WILDERNESS

After Labour's defeat in 1951, Ness stayed on Labour's Frontbench as principal spokesman on Post Office matters for nine years. In November 1951 Ness polled a respectable 43 votes in the Parliamentary Labour Party's election for its Parliamentary Committee (the Shadow Cabinet). Although well short of securing enough votes to make it into the Parliamentary Committee, it was sufficient to ensure that Ness remained in Labour's front line. Throughout this period in opposition he harassed and ripped into the Conservative Government with enthusiasm, giving the impression to some that he was perhaps more comfortable in opposition than in Government. It is debatable if this was the case; what is certain is that Ness gave the Tories a very hard time.

In a debate in the House on the Government's White Paper on Commercial Television in December 1953 Ness lambasted the Tories for having given the advertisers everything they had asked for. The White Paper was, said Ness, "a muddle to cover a fiddle". The following year saw him denouncing the Television Bill which followed as "a monstrosity" and leading a line-by-line opposition. For Ness the Government's proposals were "a great danger to the mental and cultural outlook of the people of Britain". When Labour would return to power, Ness said that it would reserve the right to "eliminate commercial advertising altogether".

Throughout the 1950s Ness maintained his opposition to the commercialisation of television. In March 1959 he complained in the House that "There are far more breaks at peak viewing time than at lower viewing time. How comes it that regularly there are more breaks and more time devoted to advertising in the peak period?" The reply from the Government was not to Ness's satisfaction. Nor did the content of the BBC's programmes escape Ness's attention. In 1958, he criticised the BBC for "dumbing down" its radio programmes in favour of more light entertainment. Then, later in the year, he drew Parliament's attention to a BBC broadcast to schools entitled "Stanley Baldwin and the General Strike of 1926". The broadcast was, he said, both biased and factually inaccurate, a "travesty of history" which would "poison" the minds of children against trade unions. It was, in short, "not education, but fabrication". Seldom a friend of the BBC, Ness on one occasion even suggested that the BBC take a "very decent dose of magnesium to get rid of the flatulence".

Ness also attacked the Tories' management of the Post Office. He claimed, in 1957, that for the first time since 1913, the Post Office was "in the red". Three revisions in the Post Office's estimates, three White Papers and changes in charges, "up one day, down the next", meant that the Post Office was in a financial mess.

In the immediate aftermath of Labour's 1951 election defeat, Ness believed that Labour would soon get back into power. Labour, after all, had a good record in Government and it was, Ness believed, only a matter of time before the electorate turned back to Labour. It was, therefore, essential that the Labour movement conducted itself responsibly so that the electorate would see Labour as a Government-in-waiting.

This is why Ness was so strongly opposed to the disruption caused by a small number of industrial militants in the early 1950s. Ness also believed that the advance of democratic socialism depended on further public ownership and he realised that in a democracy it was necessary to secure the support of people for the idea of nationalisation. If Labour's limited programme of nationalisation was not seen to be a success, then there would be little support to further "socialise" the economy. Ness believed that workers in the nationalised industries had a moral responsibility to support their industries and not to undermine them or tarnish their image in the eyes of the electorate.

Given Ness's firm views on industrial relations in the nationalised industries, it is not surprising that in the early 1950s Ness found himself at odds with the industrial militants who were creating and fuelling dissent in the nationalised industries. In particular, Ness was extremely critical of an "irresponsible minority who have benefited by the first socialist efforts and then show an arrogant indifference to the well-being of the many". These were the organisers frequently members of the Communist Party - of a wave of unofficial strikes and 'go-slows' in the nationalised industries. The coal industry suffered more than any other industry. Soon after nationalisation there had been sporadic industrial relations problems. For example, in Penallta Colliery, near Ystrad Mynach, in Ness's own constituency, there was an unofficial 'stay down' strike within a year of public ownership. But by the early 1950s the industrial action had assumed a different and more ominous character.

In an article in the *Daily Herald* in February 1953, Ness spelt out his concerns in pointed terms. Realising that miners in as many as 50 of South Wales's 159 collieries were refusing to work on Saturdays, Ness stated he knew of one colliery which had not worked on a Saturday since April 1952. Yet the wages of the men were being maintained by miners who did work on Saturdays. Moreover, Ness stated that those men who went on unofficial strike for a week, lost a week's wages and a week's output of coal but at the end of the week, wrote Ness with clear exasperation, the "men resumed work on the same conditions in order that the

56

dispute might be handled through the official channels". In a statement which could have come easily from the pen of a contemporary Labour politician, Ness asked if "In the battle to establish 'rights' have we failed adequately to stress the need for obligations?" This unofficial action, Ness said, was led by men who "condone the liquidation of anti-social elements" in Communist countries and yet organised disruption in the socialised industries in Britain. It was clear who were Ness's targets. Only two weeks later, Will Paynter, the President of the South Wales miners and a prominent Communist, told a meeting in the Rhondda that there was a need to build up a protest movement which would not only defeat the Tory cuts but also force the Conservatives out of office.

For Ness this was arrant nonsense. If miners in other coalfields behaved like the South Wales unofficial strikers "miner's wages would fall, nationalisation would be dammed, and a fatal blow would be struck against the forces of progress". Importantly, Ness also believed that industrial action against an elected Government set a dangerous precedent. If workers could take action against a Conservative Government, what was stopping employers taking action against an elected Labour Government. This was, indeed, the "folly of the few".

The Communist Party now turned its fire on Ness. The Groesfaen Miners' Lodge in Deri in the northern Rhymney Valley and part of the Caerphilly Parliamentary Constituency called for Ness's resignation as an MP. More damagingly, the Lodge Committee of the large Bedwas Colliery sent a telegram to Ness strongly objecting to his recent comments about the mines and also demanding his immediate resignation as a miners' MP. The Bedwas Lodge Committee then followed through with an open letter to the *South Wales Echo*. In it the Lodge officials criticised Ness for "condemning the miners out of hand", before concluding their letter with a demand that Ness "stop carrying the flag that lowers the miners' standards".

Ness responded by issuing an emphatic statement. "I am not to be deterred from doing my duty to the mass of miners by any threat of political victimisation … I invite the Bedwas Committee to take their decision to a full Lodge meeting at which I should have the right to speak".*

There is no evidence that such a meeting was convened, but at the Penallta Colliery a meeting of lodge members gave their MP unanimous support. Two Labour Party Wards - Hengoed and one of the Caerphilly Wards - also expressed backing for Ness's stand and the Caerphilly Divisional Labour Party passed a vote of confidence in him. Ness's position was secure and his determination to continue to be outspoken was undiminished.

*The decision to send the telegram to Ness was made at a Lodge Committee meeting attended by only 17 men.

Ness's opposition to the Communist Party in the National Union of Mineworkers (NUM) was unrelenting. In the Minutes of the Caerphilly South Ward Labour Party a remarkable attack by Ness on the Communist Party is recorded. At a meeting in January 1953, Ness warned that the Communists were making "great progress" among the trade unions, holding almost every seat on the South Wales NUM Executive. In these years Ness saw no difference between Nazism and Communism, believing that "dictators all follow the same pattern". No doubt reflecting the inside information supplied by his friend, Bill Crews, who was now General Secretary of the South Wales NUM, and strongly resisting the Communists within the union, Ness claimed that the Communist Party would stop at nothing to achieve their ends, including "manipulating" ballots.

Ness's views of Soviet Communism during the Cold War were reinforced when he visited the Soviet Union as Deputy Leader of a delegation of Peers and MPs in October 1954. The visit came at a critical time in Anglo-Soviet relations, less than 18 months after the death of Stalin. Throughout the 15 day visit the delegation received red carpet treatment from their hosts and Ness was given the privilege of making a short address to the Supreme Soviet in Moscow. On his return Ness wrote a set of quite detailed "Notes and Opinions" about his visit, focusing on the meetings and discussions he had with various Soviet luminaries. The first senior figure Ness spoke with at length was Mr. Saburov, Chairman of the Soviet Union's Economic Planning Committee, a post Ness saw as the Soviet equivalent of Chancellor of the Exchequer. When asked by Saburov, over dinner, what he thought of relations between the USSR and Britain, Ness told him that Britain wanted good relations "that could only be on the basis of non-interference with the affairs of others". Not only did that non-interference relate to affairs of state, it also applied to political and industrial activity.

No doubt with Communist activity in the nationalised industries back home in his mind, Ness told Saburov that "British social democracy would work out its own destiny in its own way, and Russian interference would only hamper us in our progress". The conversation with Saburov continued after the meal, with the Russian wanting to know of Ness what he thought the Soviet Union should do to convince the West that they really wanted peace and trade. Ness responded that the "established working class movement outside the Iron Curtain were suspicious of everything the Russians said or did". With everyone living in fear of the Soviets turning on their country next, he informed his host that Russia had lost all the ground and all the sympathy they had when they fought in Stalingrad. If this distrust was to be removed then the Soviet Union would have to make a monumental effort.

Ness then proceeded to list a number of diplomatic initiatives that the Russians could take to improve the situation - giving Austria a peace treaty; offering to disarm East Germany as a condition for not rearming West Germany; suggesting an alliance to contain Germany. But, above all else, Ness told Saburov that if the Soviet Union was to have a new approach and if it really wanted to live and let live, then they "must put in new mouths", by which Ness meant that changes in personnel were needed because, quite simply, "nobody trusts the old ones".

Ness's discussion with Saburov continued at a British Embassy reception a few days later. On this occasion, however, Ness and Saburov were joined by Molotov, the Foreign Minister.

As the group from Britain was coming to the end of its visit, Saburov asked Ness what were his "frank impressions" of the country. Ness needed little encouragement: he acknowledged that there was much in the Soviet Union that was good but expressed his view that "the priorities were wrong". Humanity was taking second place to economics, with the present being asked to sacrifice too much for the future. This he found surprising because he expected "Socialists would have been a bit more human than Capitalists".

To reinforce his point, Ness drew on his extensive knowledge of Marxism and referred to Engels's *'The Condition of the Working Class in England'*. This painted a powerful picture of exploitation and suffering and Ness wondered what Engels would have said about Russia. Socialists had a duty to mitigate the negative consequences of social adjustment and this was simply not happening in Russia.

Such remarks were too much for Molotov. He interrupted Ness to say that Russian production "was as good as any in the world". To which Ness replied that this was "nonsense". A rural peasantry could not be transformed into industrial craftsmen in one generation. The Soviet Union was "doing well" in economic terms but had not yet caught up with the countries of the West.

Not liking Ness's comments one bit, and probably being quite incensed by Ness quoting Engels at him, Molotov turned the discussion to the international situation. Ness, once again, explained how he saw things. The MP for Caerphilly said that he had gained the impression that Russia feared a united Germany, dominated by the military, more than they feared the USA. To which Molotov snarled "we shall see that Germany never again becomes a threat".

Ness's conversation then continued with Saburov and Kuznetsov, the Deputy Foreign Minister, and Ness told them candidly that he believed the USSR was responsible for the current tension in international relations:

> *After the war your tactics in Poland and Czechoslovakia shocked us all. But the arming of East Germany was the greatest mistake of all. And what you did there is what every country in Europe thinks you will do to them if you get the chance. Every country fears your tactics. You transform all your friends into your enemies.*

Kuznetsov immediately denounced Ness's remarks saying that Ness was speaking for the capitalists and that he was a typical defender of the bourgeois. Not to be outdone, Ness retorted that at least, unlike Kuznetsov, he was not a trade unionist turned into a smooth-tongued diplomat. At this point Saburov quickly intervened and snapped at Kuznetsov in Russian. According to Ness, Kuznetsov immediately "shut up" and confined himself to interpreting Saburov for the rest of the conversation. Not daunted, Ness continued to criticise the entire basis of Soviet foreign policy and Saburov changed the conversation onto an area he felt more comfortable, the "success" of the Soviet planned economy.

The conversation between Ness and Saburov and Kuznetsov was resumed at a reception given by the Chairman of the Council of Ministers on another night. This time, however, the conversation did not get so heated and the Russian hosts made, it would seem, a very conscious effort to charm their guests and impress upon them their determination to build good international relations. But this did not stop Ness having his say. He told his Soviet hosts that while "everything depended upon good relations, the antics of some of the Communist Party [in Britain] did not help because what the CP did in Britain was ascribed to Russian influence". Then, in no uncertain terms, Ness told Saburov and Kuznetsov "let the British working class work out its own destiny in its own way … British problems could only be solved in Britain. Russia couldn't export solutions on the class struggle". The British working class had more experience of dealing with the issue of class than the Russians and, Ness assured his hosts, the British working class knew what it was doing.

Despite his strong words, Ness believed the meeting concluded "in an atmosphere of great friendliness". Ness told Saburov that if he lived in Britain he would be a "good Social Democrat" and Saburov returned the back-handed compliment by telling Ness that if he lived in Russian he would be a "good Communist". Not best pleased, Ness retorted "you will live to see Russia a social democracy yet". Determined to have the last word, Saburov left Ness with the words "only the strong can be generous".

On the final day of the visit the delegation went to the Kremlin to meet Malenkov, the Prime Minister. They were ushered into his long room and he came down half way to meet his guests. With him was Molotov. For over an hour the delegation discussed with their hosts what long term co-existence meant in practise; how peaceful co-existence between countries of different systems could be guaranteed; and how trade and other forms of co-operation, like student exchanges, could be extended.

For Ness, this last meeting was particularly cordial and it helped him to conclude that the essence of Russian policy consisted of three elements, which in some ways were contradictory. First, Ness believed that there was a "deep desire" to build up the economy and that the economic planners were of the opinion that the military demands upon manpower and resources were holding back the rate of economic progress. Secondly, Ness believed that the experience of the Second World War still weighed heavily on the Russian consciousness. The Soviet Union had, of course, suffered more than any other nation and "never again shall we be caught unprepared" was a refrain which the delegation had heard time and again. That fear of history repeating itself led the Russian military to see the potential for aggression all around its national borders. The Russians had built up a gigantic military force because of fear. In response, NATO had been created and Western Europe had been rearmed and, in turn, this had created fresh fear amongst the Soviets. The only way to break this "vicious spiral" was through decisive action. Ness therefore proposed a summit between Malenkov, Churchill and Eisenhower with the aim of ending "the dangerous drift" towards a conflict which nobody wanted.

But thirdly, Ness was left under no illusion that the obligation the Russians felt towards the international working class movement meant that the Cominform* and Communist Parties in individual countries were indeed instruments of Russian policy. Ness's view that the Communist Party of Great Britain was a tool of Russian interest was confirmed: it was nothing less than "a fifth column".

On a very different note, when back in Britain, Ness drafted an article which he entitled 'A Woman at the Top in Moscow'. In it Ness explained that when in Moscow he met a woman who was the leader of the Moscow Communist Party. She was married to the Russian Ambassador to Yugoslavia and they had six children. According to Ness, she was a typical Russian woman in that she was "well padded in her middle". In conversation he apparently told her bluntly that "feminine beauty would not get a chance when the women had all the dirty jobs to do sweeping the roads, making the roads, labouring on its buildings and digging the holes for the men to put in the electric pylons". He also told his host that it was only in the theatre that the delegation had seen "beautiful women".

Later in the visit he again met the same Russian woman, only on this occasion it was at a banquet rather than in a formal meeting. Now the woman had put on a little face powder and some lipstick and she made a point of telling Ness that she had done so. Nevertheless, Ness was not impressed. Her simple clothes made her look "more like an average housewife than a highly successful Communist functionary". For Ness it would appear that socialism did not have a feminist dimension.

The following year Ness went to East Germany and in 1956 he visited Yugoslavia as Deputy Leader of a Parliamentary delegation. In contrast to the Soviet Union

*The Cominform was the Soviet dominated Communist Information Bureau.

and East Germany, Ness was extremely impressed with what he found in the Republic of Yugoslavia and concluded that the country was "the best expression of Socialism in the modern world". From the handwritten notes which Ness made for two public lectures which he delivered on his return, it is possible to see that Ness was impressed with a number of features in Tito's Yugoslavia. These included the way the Federal structure of government enabled a wide range of ethnic groups to live together; the fact that, even though the country was far from prosperous, in industry and agriculture, especially through co-operatives, great material advances were being made; and Ness was impressed by the decentralisation of decision making so that, he believed, the State was, as Marx predicted, "withering away". With the benefit of hindsight it is easy to see that Ness's optimism about Yugoslavia was not well founded but at the time it was a view shared by many on the democratic left.

Ness's critical views about the absence of democracy in the USSR and the subservient role of the British Communist Party to its Soviet "masters" meant that Ness found himself embroiled in often heated debates with those on the left of the Labour Party who saw Soviet Communism through rose-tinted spectacles. Far from seeing Khrushchev as a more 'liberal' leader, Ness, as we have seen, was far more critical and events in Hungary, especially, were to prove him correct. Ness's trenchant criticism of the Soviet Union was, in large part, shared by Aneurin Bevan. In the pages of 'In Place of Fear', Bevan, for example, was highly critical of the absence of democracy in the Soviet Union, even referring to Soviet Communism on one occasion as the "running mate" of fascism. Ness and Nye's shared analysis arose from the fact that they both held firm to the same democratic socialist values.

Ness Edwards and Aneurin Bevan, of course, knew each other extremely well: they had had a common political apprenticeship, attending the Marxist Central Labour College together; both represented Valley seats in South East Wales and, as ex-miners, both Ness and Nye were sponsored by the NUM. The two men shared a common political philosophy. They believed in the necessity for common ownership, linked to industrial democracy, and they saw internationalism as being central to their vision of a better world, making them both strong opponents of Welsh nationalism. And yet the two men were very different individuals. Ness was very well aware of how their personalities differed. In a beautifully written tribute to Nye after his premature death in 1960, Ness threw a penetrative light on Bevan's personality when he wrote how, when at the Labour College, he realised that Nye's mind "had the speed of a racehorse", and no matter how much he neglected 'set works' he could always pick up arguments and race ahead of his fellow students. In that tribute in the *South Wales Argus*, Ness wrote how, at College, Nye tended to argue with his fellow students through the night and would then stay in bed until midday and miss many of his lectures. Ness recalled Nye explaining that "he could not settle down to work because he was like a bee" and wanted "the nectar from many flowers". This was the essence of Nye, "he wanted to taste all that life could give". It was true when they were at the Labour College and it was true throughout his life.

Here was, perhaps, an inkling of the real difference between Ness and Nye. While Ness was an intense, serious and studious man, who loved being at home in Caerphilly with his wife and five children, Nye was very different. He was renowned for his cutting humour, his volatile temperament and his distain for 'academic discipline'. Nye and his wife, Jennie Lee, were a strong political partnership whose lives were focused on London rather than South Wales. Nye also enjoyed the finer things in life. He appreciated good food and wine and frequently socialised with people who were as far removed from the working class as one could imagine. This helped to explain why Nye was an infrequent visitor to the Welsh table in the House of Commons' tearoom and why Ness, privately at least, saw him as something of a 'Bollinger Bolshevik'.

The differences in personality and lifestyle between the two men did not mean that Ness failed to recognise Bevan's genius or the importance of his greatest achievement, the National Health Service, but it did mean there was a certain distance between the two MPs. This distance provided a space for a number of political disagreements to emerge and these may well have been accentuated by Jennie Lee. She, it has been alleged, had an unfortunate tendency to patronise fellow MPs and Ness, of all people, did not take kindly to being patronised by anyone.

In the early 1950s especially, the relationship between Ness and Nye was particularly strained. In 1951, Nye resigned from the Labour Government because he objected to the introduction of NHS prescription charges. Ness believed that Nye's resignation was a mistake. While he had some sympathy with Nye's 'principled stand' (he believed that the money which had to be found could have been raised through savings in administration), nevertheless, Ness's view was that once Party policy had been agreed by the Cabinet it should have been adhered to.

Adding fuel to the Bevan fire was a small group of left wing Labour MPs who became known as the "Bevanites", although association with Nye was not always as close as many assumed. "Middle class intellectuals" like Barbara Castle, Richard Crossman, Ian Mikado, and the journalist, Michael Foot, were not Ness's natural 'soul mates' and by October 1952, Ness was becoming increasingly exasperated with their efforts to take the Labour Party in a more left wing direction. Ness was particularly antagonistic to the Bevanites' opposition to rearmament. For Ness, as we have seen, the Soviet Union was not merely an undemocratic State, it was also a very real threat to the West.

In October 1952, Ness went around the Labour Party wards in the Caerphilly Division to put the case against the Bevanites. Without a formal invitation, Ness went to a meeting of the influential Bargoed ward; Ness said he had called in "to see how the Party is really functioning". Ness then went on to express his concern about differences in the Party and explained that "Mr. Churchill had referred to Clem Atlee as one leader of the Labour Party and Mr. Aneurin Bevan as the other". In Ness's view many of the differences were of a personal nature and the rank-and-file had to weigh-up what they heard from Aneurin with the necessity to be "loyal to the Party". He urged members not to engage in "hero worship or personal hatred". If there was any "organising done outside the Party he would oppose it as ruthless[ly] as he could".

On the following night Ness went to a meeting of the Caerphilly South Ward Labour Party. Here he let his feelings be known in no uncertain terms. Ness explained to Party members that, in his view, the left wing *Tribune* newspaper had become "the official organ of a Party within a Party". The dissent inside the Labour Party had reached such an extent that he now believed that "If people in the Party could not agree with the Party policy and could not work with the orthodox section of the Party they should be expelled".

Uproar ensued, with heated exchanges continuing after the meeting. Unusually, these are recorded in the Ward Minutes. One Party member commented that he had never heard "so much disaffection" expressed after a meeting and that Ness ought to remember "that 89%" of the rank-and-file shared Bevan's views. Ominously, that same Party member added that Ness Edwards "must remember that he is not in an unassailable position".

At a Divisional Party Executive meeting in the same month, there was a full discussion of the Bevanite controversy in the Party. It would appear to have been a tense meeting and, according to one of the delegates from Bargoed, Ness seemed "a worried man" when he addressed the meeting. As it turned out, there was no reason for Ness to be overly concerned. The Executive mandated Ness to vote in the Parliamentary Labour Party for the disbanding of all groups, "including the Bevan group". It was also made clear that, if the resolution was not accepted, then "Aneurin Bevan and his 30 followers should be expelled from the Parliamentary Labour Party".

Despite the strong feelings in the Parliamentary Labour Party (PLP) and the Party as a whole, no expulsions occurred, but Nye Bevan and the Bevanites continued to be a thorn in the side of the leadership throughout most of the 1950s. As a consequence, Ness's relationship with Nye continued to be quite distant.

During the dark Tory years of the 1950s, as well as being Labour's spokesman on the Post Office, Ness also took a keen interest in a whole range of other issues. He was forthright in his condemnation of Prime Minister Anthony Eden for the invasion of Suez in 1956, warning of an Arab "Holy War"; he totally condemned the Soviet invasion of Hungary in the same year; he embraced nuclear energy with enthusiasm, arguing that an atomic energy plant should be built in Mid Wales to serve the industries of South Wales and the Midlands; and he championed the case for a bridge across the river Severn. In fact, of all the Welsh MPs Ness was the most vocal in support of a Severn Bridge which, he believed, had the potential to transform the economy of South Wales. During the inter-war years there had been no need for a bridge of this kind but now, wrote Ness in January 1958, the nature of the South Wales economy had changed and the new industries were generating an unprecedented volume of traffic. The economic arguments in favour of the Severn Bridge were overwhelming. There would be an estimated 3,000 lorries using the bridge every day, "saving 6,000 man hours per day", plus savings in "petrol, wear and tear, tyres, oil, etc., and the greater efficiency in the use of transport". In total, Ness estimated there would be a saving for industry of between £7 million and £10 million per year.

The Severn Bridge was opened on 8 September 1966, its construction due in no small part to Ness's persistent and vigorous campaign. It was, however, a campaign which was not always warmly supported by his fellow Welsh MPs. In February 1956 Ness's colleagues in the All-Party Welsh Parliamentary Party even went so far as to pass a Motion of Censure on him because he supported the principle of a toll system on the bridge, the need for which had been widely accepted by this time. The Motion of Censure, thought Ness, was initiated and supported by MPs who did not reside in the area and who hoped, wrongly, that by obstructing the bridge extra money would be available for projects in other parts of Wales. Such disunity may have been why, when the Government considered the ease of Parliamentary passage, it gave priority to the bridge across the Firth of Forth over the Severn Bridge.

Apart from his Frontbench responsibilities and the issues and campaigns about which Ness felt passionate, throughout much of the 1950s Ness was preoccupied with one profound and all-pervading subject. He was concerned about the *kind* of socialism the Labour Party should be seeking to create and the direction in which the Party was moving. In 1956 the Fabian intellectual, Anthony Crosland, published his influential book *'The Future of Socialism'*. In it he argued for a "revision" of the Labour Party's historic view that socialism should come about through a progressive extension of public ownership. Instead, Crosland and the revisionists wanted the Labour Party to accept the desirability of a mixed economy with nationalisation being introduced only when it was deemed necessary.

At the same time the Bevanites were arguing that widespread public ownership was the only foundation upon which socialism could be built. Aneurin Bevan had published his book *'In Place of Fear'* and through the *Tribune* newspaper the left in the Party, with significant support from activists in the constituency parties, was making the case for radical policies at home and a realignment of Britain's foreign relationships. Britain, it was argued, was too close to the United States and too antagonistic towards the Soviet Union.

Philosophically Ness did not fall easily into either camp. As we have seen, in the early 1950s Ness was exasperated at the activities of the Bevanites and adopted a far more critical position on the Soviet Union than many on the left. And yet, although he was seen by some as a right-winger, especially when he was a Government Minister, Ness could never properly be described as being on the 'right' of the Labour Party.

To understand Ness's politics it is necessary to appreciate the profound impact which the Central Labour College had on him. The College had given Ness the theoretical tools to analyse and understand the world and a faith in the ability of the working class to change that world. While political action was vitally important, the industrial power and the organisation of the working class itself was essential. Socialism was the goal and it would be achieved when public ownership of the economy had been brought about through Parliamentary democracy and each industry was run in the interest of the workers and the country as a whole.

His profound commitment to "industrial unionism" and, in his youth certainly, quasi-syndicalism made Ness highly suspicious of the Communist Party. As a young man Ness resented the elitism of the communists who, he believed, put the interests of themselves, as the revolutionary vanguard, before the interests of both the unions and the working class. Whether it was the struggle against Company Unionism in the 1930s or politically inspired unofficial strikes in the 1950s, Ness strongly opposed the Communist Party for its warped principles and unsavoury practices. His longstanding hostility to the Communist Party meant, as Leo Abse, the former MP for Pontypool, has remarked, Ness saw through the mask of Communist rhetoric and was able to see the reality of Soviet Communism well before most of Labour's left.

If, politically, Ness was at odds with the Communist Party and the "actually existing" socialism of the USSR, and was temperamentally different to the Bevanites, he was also a long way from Labour's right wing and became increasingly distanced as the 1950s progressed. In the mid 1950s Ness had become more and more critical of Clem Attlee's leadership of the Labour Party and, according to the Labour grandee of the time, Hugh Dalton, Ness was in favour of approaching Attlee to step down from the leadership of the Party at the end of October 1955. It is not entirely clear who Ness wanted to become leader in place of Attlee, but since the days when George Brown had been Parliamentary Private Secretary to Ness, the MP for Caerphilly had maintained a close friendship with him, particularly through the highly influential trade union group. By the end of 1955 Brown had joined the camp of Hugh Gaitskell. In December of that year

Attlee did in fact step down from the leadership and, following a ballot of Labour MPs, Hugh Gaitskell was elected Leader, defeating Herbert Morrison and Aneurin Bevan. Ness, it seems, cast his vote for Gaitskell. In the more closely fought election for Deputy Leader of the Party between Jim Griffiths and Aneurin Bevan, Ness followed his Frontbench colleagues and cast his vote for Griffiths.

But this did not place Ness in the camp of Labour's right. There is no doubt that Ness had strong reservations about the revisionist ideas which were clearly gaining support in the Party. In particular, Ness was to grow increasingly suspicious of a group of right wing Labourites close to Gaitskell and frequently referred to as the "Hampstead Set". And, although in Gaitskell he might have initially seen a figure who could have propelled Labour quickly back to power, Ness soon saw things differently.

In an attempt to map out a way forward for Labour and democratic socialism which was neither Bevanite nor revisionist, Ness began work on a new book. The essential aim of this book was to examine how a socialised economy could be run accountably with the full support of ordinary people. True to his Marxist roots, Ness believed that the key to socialist progress was public ownership but it had to be a form of ownership which was truly 'accountable'. Nor was Ness concerned only with Britain and the West, he also believed that the Soviet model of ownership and control had profound weaknesses and that it, too, had to be examined critically and infused with democratic accountability. Amongst Ness's papers is the incomplete draft of six Chapters of a short book, four in type and two handwritten. The book has no title but, from the references in the text, the Chapters would appear to have been written in the late 1950s.

In the opening Chapter, under the heading 'Accountability', Ness outlined the "problem" which beset developed and developing societies across the world, both East and West. Everywhere, Ness argued, there was an unrestrained trend towards ever larger units of production. In the West this was creating huge rises in the standard of living and now, at least in material terms, there was the real possibility of a "golden age".

Monopoly by the State was increasingly seen as a necessary development in the West and the same was true of developing countries like India, China and Egypt. It was, of course, the case that in the Soviet Union large scale public ownership was already the norm and centralised planning was transforming the lives of ordinary citizens.

Yet, despite the obvious material successes of nationalisation, in every country in which the public sector had taken a more leading role there was a "failure" to give the citizen any say in the administration of the public sector. The result was that "in every country of the world" there was a real possibility that people would become:

...citizens without a purpose. In all our efforts for the welfare of the people we are in danger of doing for them everything that matters materially, each one doing his allotted work [so that there was] life without purpose.

The "problem" which Ness identified, and which he sought to address in the pages which followed, was whether a high standard of living could be achieved "whilst at the same time giving to the individual citizen the sense of feeling something more than a cipher in the complex society in which he lives". For Ness, the importance of this fundamental issue could not be underestimated. In the modern State, power was moving away from the individual with decisions about what happens in a locality being increasing made outside of that locality. This was happening to such an extent that local democratic bodies were losing their power and becoming little more "ghosts". Not only was this undesirable, it also presented a serious threat to the very fabric of democracy. "A public enterprise managerial oligarchy", wrote Ness, "can be more dangerous to democracy than even a private enterprise managerial oligarchy". The ultimate threat was the creation of a "new despotism".

The second Chapter focussed on two examples of how services operated effectively in Britain with proper accountability. The first example was one Ness knew well, the Post Office. Here, Ness explained, the Postmaster General appointed by the Prime Minister was fully "answerable to Parliament". In the Post Office the accounts were subject to annual review by MPs, as were the estimates of future expenditure. Before any capital investment in the Post Office, there had to be the prior consent of the House of Commons. Moreover, if a member of the public had a grievance about a Post Office service, a question could be asked of the Postmaster General by the individual's MP or the matter could ultimately be raised on the floor of the House of Commons. The Post Office Board sat regularly and advised the Postmaster General on policy decisions and the day-to-day running of the Post Office's activities was in the hands of a management structure headed by the Director General. Ness believed that the operation of the service in this way was a good example of a public service being carried out "under the seeing eyes of the citizen".

The other example cited by Ness was an unusual one, the Armed Forces. Ness argued that the Navy, Army and Airforce were each run differently but, at the end of the day, there was direct accountability to Parliament for decisions taken and money spent. The Public Accounts Committee had a particularly important role in scrutinising expenditure.

In the third Chapter, Ness began by referring to the Second Reading debate in the House on the Bill of 1933 which established a Board to manage and organise the relief of the unemployed. During the debate most contributors focussed exclusively on the hardship that would be caused in the mining communities but Aneurin

Bevan also had some perceptive things to say about the constitutional precedent which the Bill was setting. Ness quoted Nye extensively when he pointed out that the Bill disenfranchised British citizens because it was taking away from Ministers the responsibility for individual cases. The Bill, said Nye, was undermining Parliamentary democracy and, as such, would be seen in retrospect as "a milestone upon the road to fascism in Great Britain". It was a Bill, Nye claimed, that would make the poor "dumb".

Ness agreed strongly with the assessment of the Member for Ebbw Vale. The Assistance Board had indeed been established as a body independent of both Ministers and Parliament and, as a result, elected MPs were unable to raise the treatment being meted out to individuals because responsibility rested elsewhere.

When Labour was elected in 1945 the same model that had been used for the Assistance Board was used for the newly nationalised industries, Ness explained. The Prime Minister set up a committee of Ministers, under the chairmanship of Herbert Morrison, to examine how best to run the industries that were to be taken into public ownership. What resulted was the "Morrisonian Doctrine of the Public Corporation". It was decreed that the running of each industry was to be in the hands of an appointed Board which would be, as Morrison himself stated, free from Parliamentary pressure and the indirect pressure of the constituents of MPs. In other words, the model of the Unemployment Assistance Board had been extended.

This model of public ownership Ness objected to strongly. He saw it as both undemocratic and dangerous and he particularly resented Morrison's suggestion, in his book *'Government and Parliament'*, that Ministers should exercise influence on industries' Boards by informal methods. This was a recipe for Ministers becoming "unresponsible to Parliament". If this was the Ministers' preferred method of exercising influence, then Board Chairmen, whose re-appointment depended on Ministerial patronage, would willingly accept this but the Minister, as a result, would escape from having any accountability to Parliament.

The growth of the unaccountable administrative machine was not, Ness explained in Chapter 4, a new phenomenon: the struggle to ensure appropriate democratic control was part of the historic confrontation between King and Parliament and then between Ministers of the Crown and Parliament and, most recently, between the Government Executive and Parliament. In 1934, with the creation of the Unemployment Assistance Board, that age old struggle had merely taken on a new form.

Ness analysed the Report of the Haldane Committee of 1918 on the Machinery of Government and found in it much to be commended. He also referred to the work of Fred Jowitt, one of the leaders of the ILP, who argued in the late 1920s that there should be a Standing Committee of Members appointed for each Government

Department. As the problem of accountability had become more acute, the House had had the good sense to establish a Select Committee on national expenditure.

During the Second World War, as State intervention and organisation increased dramatically, a special Select Committee was established to scrutinise Government expenditure, but at the end of the war the Committee was wound up. However, in 1952 the Commons appointed a Select Committee on the nationalised industries to examine the whole issue of accountability. The Committee's terms of reference were to examine how the House of Commons was currently informed about the affairs of the nationalised industries and to report on what changes might be desirable so that accountability could be extended.

To Ness's disappointment, the Committee in its report accepted Morrison's argument that no Select Committee could ask questions of Ministers on topics which were outside of the responsibility of their particular industries. On this Morrison had been supported, predictably, by all the Chairmen of the Boards who gave evidence. Nevertheless, the Committee did agree that there ought to be a permanent Committee of the House to inform Parliament about "the aims, activities and problems of the corporations".

Despite the recommendations of the Committee, to Ness's anger the TUC and the PLP opposed the creation of such a permanent committee, believing there was no case for it. Herbert Morrison, now Deputy Leader of the Labour Party, came forward with a "rehash of usual opposition to any change"; an attitude which came to be summarised, said Ness, by the words "leave it to the boss". The Government of the day, however, supported the recommendations and a new permanent Select Committee on the nationalised industries was duly established in March 1955. Six months later the Committee produced a report arguing for an expansion of its terms of reference to include the ability to examine detailed aspects of the industries' finances. A great step forward had been taken for democracy and accountability.

Elsewhere in his draft, Ness set out some of the other democratic reforms which he thought were necessary in Britain. "The first step", he argued, had to be the reorganisation of the House of Commons. Apart from in depth scrutiny through appropriate and effective Select Committees, Ness attached great importance "to the interrogation of Ministers" at Question Time. This, Ness believed, was vital for accountability but it needed to be made more effective. To achieve this he thought that Departmental Questions should be held more regularly and changes introduced to the then system of determining how many questions a Member could ask.

The other two draft Chapters, 5 and 7 (there is no Chapter 6), are written in infuriatingly small handwritten notes. Both Chapters are concerned mainly with the Soviet Union and its profound shortcomings. Ness's draft of Chapter 5 begins with the chilling statement "Non-accountability for the exercise of political power finds its logical result in the 'cult of the personality' and all the barbarity of

Stalinism'. For Ness the fundamental failings of the Soviet Union lay not with the personality. The fault lay with the 'system' which allowed Stalin to become such a vile dictator. The Russian Marxists would not blame Anthony Eden, the British Prime Minister, for the failure of the capitalist economy, said Ness, and yet they ascribe so many of Russia's recent horrors to Stalin's personal weaknesses. The experience of the Soviet Union had to be an example, and a warning, to all democracies and all democrats. "The theory of the dictatorship of the proletariat goes by the board when the dictatorship shoots the proletariat".

Chapter 7 entitled 'The People's Democracies' goes even further in its condemnation of the Soviet Union. Throughout Eastern Europe, Ness was to remind readers, communism only existed because it had been imposed by the Soviet Union. The tyranny of Stalin had seen the Soviet State develop all the characteristics of an absolute monarchy "with all the worst features of Czarism exercised by an uncrowned king". Although Ness did acknowledge that the USSR had made great economic progress, without having any way of knowing the true magnitude of Stalin's genocide, Ness, unlike so many on the British left, categorically stated that the price in human suffering to achieve economic progress was completely unacceptable.

It was no surprise, suggested Ness, that the criticism of Stalin occurred only after his death. But, apart from this condemnation of Stalin when it was safe to do so, what if anything, asked Ness, had changed in the Soviet Union. Had the men in the Kremlin become subject to any institutional checks? What was there to stop a new Stalin emerging? Ness's view was that the famous Khrushchev speech of February 1956 to the Twentieth Communist Party Congress, in which the crimes of Stalin were denounced, had changed little. The fundamental weaknesses in the Soviet system of government had not been addressed and there was hardly anything to suggest that they were going to be. The 'party line' was still being issued from the top, without consultation, "transforming men into sheep". Stalin had used the machinery of the "old Bolsheviks" to achieve his ends and Khrushchev himself had had his main rival, Beria, executed. Democracy in the Soviet Union was a sham, people did not enjoy freedom of speech and in elections they were able to vote only for approved candidates.

Nevertheless, Ness's belief in the efficacy of public ownership convinced him that the USSR, in spite of everything, had "laid the basis for a new form of society". Developing countries were looking for models on which to base their development; some were looking at the Soviet Union, others were looking to the West, while a third group was wanting "the best of both worlds". In Ness's opinion, this was the way forward: the planned, nationalised economy of the Soviets, and the political, democratic practices of the West. Such a "third way" meant rejecting the "anarchy of capitalism" and "the slavery of the totalitarian state".

How the Daily Express saw Ness's resignation from the Labour Frontbench.

Ness believed both East and West had to change. The Soviet Union's Supreme Soviet had to meet regularly: elections should be open, with individuals being freely nominated and elected on a frequent basis: as well as Communist Party candidates, Ness believed that non-Party and even anti-Party people should be allowed to put their names forward for election: and then the all-important Praesidium should be fully accountable to the Supreme Soviet. In addition, Ness believed the Russians should "devolve" power out of Moscow to the national Soviets. While Ness fell short of advocating a multi-Party democracy, nevertheless this was the inexorable logic of his argument.

Sadly, Ness failed to complete the book. If it had been finished and had reached the book-shelves it would have been a significant contribution to Labour thinking at a critical period in its history. As it is, Ness's notes serve to provide us with a fascinating insight into Ness' views on some of the most profound issues of the day.

While Ness's opinions on the democratic failings of the Soviet Union antagonised some of Labour's left, Ness's criticism of Morrisonian-style public corporations and his total commitment to accountable public ownership, meant there was a widening chasm, too, between Ness and some of the revisionists. After Labour's defeat in the General Election of September 1959, the voices of the revisionists became stronger and, with the unpublicised blessing of Hugh Gaitskell, an initiative was taken to redefine the whole nature of the Labour Party. Douglas Jay MP proposed that there should be an end to further nationalisation, that MPs ought to have more influence in the Party, and the trade unions less, and that the Labour Party should even change its name. No longer should the Labour Party be a working class Party, with an old fashioned, "cloth cap" image but, instead, Jay and the other "radicals" argued, Labour should be transformed into a modern social democratic Party. For Ness, such ideas were sacrilege. They offended everything he stood for and believed in throughout his entire trade union and political career. Although Gaitskell did not seek to impose all of Jay's ideas on the Party, and in the end the Leader of the Opposition backed away from trying to drop Clause IV of the Party's constitution, the commitment to public ownership, nevertheless, under Gaitskell the Party was moving in a clearly revisionist direction. The one man who seemed the only person able, or in a position, to curb Gaitskell's modernising excesses was Aneurin Bevan.

Towards the end of the 1950s Ness and Nye seemed to have had a closer political relationship. As we have seen, they shared similar views on Welsh nationalism and the debate in the Party about Labour's fundamental principles gave the two men firm common ground. But in 1959 Nye developed cancer and in the following July he passed away. To Ness it must have seemed like there was little that could be done to hold back Gaitskell and the 'Hampstead Set'. It was, therefore, of little surprise that at the end of July 1960 Ness issued a statement saying that he had

73

informed the Chief Whip that he no longer wished to continue serving the Leader of the Party as Labour's principal Frontbench spokesman on Post Office matters. Ness explained that there was no question of him disagreeing with any point of Labour policy. He had made his decision, he said, because, at the age of 63 and having been the Party's opposition spokesman on the Post Office for nine years, he felt the time had come to "make way for a younger man". No doubt Ness was not as sprightly as he once was but the MP for Caerphilly judged that this was not the time to disclose the main reason for his resignation. This was explained over four months later to the *Western Mail* which carried a story about Ness's reasons for resignation on its front page:

> *Since the General Election I have had considerable apprehension about the efforts of a small but influential group in the Party to emasculate the fundamental principles of the Movement. Last July I decided that I could not continue to accept the restraints which a Shadow job imposed.*

Ness, in that same interview, stated that he now felt much more free to express himself "on matters which I feel will concern the deeper purposes of the Movement". In fact, Ness had already started to do precisely that, well before his interview with the *Western Mail* in December 1960. At the Labour Party Conference in the autumn of that year the Conference delegates voted by a small majority in favour of unilateral nuclear disarmament. Gaitskell, however, had responded by stating emphatically that he would not accept the decision but would "fight, fight, and fight again" to save the Party he loved. Ness was aghast and made it clear that he could no longer support a leadership that regarded acceptance of Party Conference decisions to be a crime. And warning his colleagues in the PLP, Ness said that it would be "political suicide" for the Parliamentary Party to refuse to take into account the decisions of Conference. "None of us is big enough to set ourselves above the Movement", he told his fellow Labour MPs and a wider audience in the Labour movement. "While Labour MPs are not the delegates of the Party in Westminster, neither, while they are Members of the Party, are they entitled to disregard and in some cases openly defy the Party decisions". The response of Hugh Gaitskell to the unilateralist vote confirmed to Ness that he was right in resigning from the Frontbench.

Such forthright comments brought swift and harsh criticism from Ness's fellow Valleys Labour MPs, a group traditionally loyal to the Party leadership. Iorwerth Thomas, MP for Rhondda West, was typical of many when he stated that Ness Edwards ought to "keep his mouth shut" until the Parliamentary Party had met and "should not engage in public political brawls". In contrast, Ness's local Divisional Party declared that it was firmly behind its MP. The local Party met, discussed the developments with Ness, and agreed to issue a public statement. Ness's Agent, Cllr. D. G. Evans, declared, without equivocation, that "we as a Divisional Party are completely behind Mr. Edwards". Ness's time at the frontline of British politics had come to an end. A new period though had already begun.

Ness and his wife outside the Labour Committee rooms during the 1939 By-Election.

Ness with wife and young family.

Ness standing at a gallows in Buchenwald.

Ness and Mavis Tate MP see some of the bodies being taken away.

The British MPs witness the true horror of Buchenwald. Outside hut 61 they see the bodies of those who had died that morning.

At his desk as the recently appointed Postmaster General in 1950.

Ness at the Bolshoi Theatre in Moscow.

Marshal Tito with the Delegation of British Parliamentarians in 1958.

Ness with the principal guests at Caerphilly R.F.C's Annual Dinner.

Ness Edwards with Parliamentary colleagues Tudor Watkins MP, Ivor Davies MP, Parliamentary Under Secretary of State for Wales and Michael Foot MP. Taken at the opening of the Heads of the Valleys Road.

Harman Nicholls MP meets the press at Caerphilly Castle. Also in the photograph are Civil Servants, representatives of Caerphilly UDC and Ness.

Ness proudly welcomes Harold Wilson, the Prime Minister, to Caerphilly to open the Harold Wilson Industrial Estate in March 1966.

Ness talking to a group of schoolchildren from Caerphilly on the House of Common Terrace in 1967.

Ness at the 6th Annual Dinner of the Bargoed Branch of the AEU in 1967. To Ness's right is Bill Coleman; to his left is John Haydn Jones, Vice Chairman of Gelligaer UDC, Bill Lewis, a former miner then working at the Austin plant at Tir-y-Berth, and Cllr. Eric Evans, Bedwellty.

Unveiling of the plaque in Bargoed to commemorate Ness's life-time of service. The plaque reads :"Erected in appreciation of the Services Rendered to the community by Ness Edwards PC, Member of Parliament 1939-1968, Postmaster General 1950-1951". In the photograph are, from left to right, Fred Evans MP, Ness's children, Anne Mitchel, Alan Edwards, and Margaret Jenkins. Then Mrs Evans and Ness's two other children, Rhys Edwards and Llin Golding. Closest to the plaque are Cllr. Brin Harris, Chairman of Gelligaer UDC, and Mrs Edwards.

CHAPTER 5

THE NATIONAL QUESTION
AND THE CAERPHILLY DOCTRINE

Ness was a patriotic Welshman and an internationalist. Throughout his life he had a confident pride in his native country and believed there was no contradiction in being Welsh, British, European and an internationalist. In fact, Ness believed that one of the key characteristics of modern Wales was its ability to look out to the world and not in on itself.

Ness's definition of Welshness was not based on the Welsh language. He recognised that in the Wales of the Twentieth Century the Welsh language was only one of the ingredients which made the country what it was. The language should be respected and nurtured but it should not become the preserve of an elite. His views on the language were always controversial in Wales and Ness was frequently the target of attacks from reactionary, nationalist elements within the Welsh speaking establishment.

In August 1950 the National Eisteddfod came to Caerphilly.* Until that year the Eisteddfod had been conducted in both English and Welsh but, for the first time, it was agreed that the Eisteddfod in Caerphilly was to implement the all-Welsh rule. From 1950 on, the Welsh language was to be the only language to be permitted on the Eisteddfod stage. As the local MP, Ness was invited, as per custom, to deliver a presidential address. Until the day before he was due to speak, it was Ness's intention to deliver his speech half in Welsh and half in English. However, he began delivering his speech in English by explaining why he had decided to give his speech entirely in English. Ness told his audience that he had made his decision after he had heard an adjudicator criticising the enunciation of a North Wales competitor. To speak entirely in English was, said Ness, "more in keeping with the dignity of the Eisteddfod".

Ness's opening remarks were greeted with a mixture of jeering and applause. Apart from the fact that he was delivering his speech entirely in English, there were elements of controversy in his speech from beginning to end. He began with a blunt attack on the all-Welsh rule, combined with a plea for Welsh National unity:

*The Gorsedd Stones are today still in the David Williams Park, overlooking Caerphilly Castle.

It will be a sad day when the people of Gwent and Rhymney are shut out from this great national festival. It will be terrible to feel that an iron curtain has been dropped between us and the National Eisteddfod. It will be a strange experience to feel that we are strangers in our own native land. Our conception of life and what it means is your conception; our regard for home and hearth is the same as yours. We are the same flesh and blood.

The second point Ness made was that cultural prosperity depended on economic success. And to secure such a transformation, rather than rely solely on outside assistance, the people of Wales should have more faith in themselves:

Because of the hard road which the people of the South Wales valleys had travelled in the first half of the century, buffeted by all the miseries and misfortunes and poverty laying over the land like a blight, Welsh leadership had to devote itself to the task of bringing succour to the people. The men of the valleys had to wrestle with a poverty that was killing Wales and her people. Now there are more smiles in Wales than for half a century. There is more hope and very much more security from a soul-killing poverty. We must remember that the greatest enemy of culture is poverty, especially the poverty we saw in South Wales in the 20's and 30's when our children were driven away. Some of the black spots had not yet been wiped out. There was still much to be done. But too often have I heard the clamour to bring in from outside new industries. I wish we could get rid of some of this self-pity and let our own native genius assert itself. Cannot we look to ourselves a bit more for the solution to our problems?

Finally, Ness returned to the issue of the all-Welsh rule, without mincing his words:

It would be a great tragedy for Wales if the predominantly English speaking areas are transformed into Welsh Sudetenlands, shut out of all things Welsh by a barrier of our own creation. It is an old controversy that cannot be settled in an atmosphere of bitterness. The road to progress is one of peace, persuasion, example and kindly toleration. We shall slip, and slip badly, if this Eisteddfod of Wales ceases to represent the whole of the people of Wales. Once it becomes a preserve for a minority or coterie none will heed it and the one thing that keeps us all together will have gone from us. We quarrel far too much among ourselves. That may be inevitable, but let us keep the National Eisteddfod as a meeting ground for all.

The conclusion of the speech was greeted with a mixture of jeering and applause. In the view of the *Merthyr Express*, Ness's speech and that of the Lord Mayor of

76

Cardiff, who also spoke in English, "threw lumps of fat into the linguistic fire". Never before had the case in favour of a bilingual Eisteddfod been delivered in English in such a persuasive and effective manner from the Eisteddfod stage. Nor was Ness's stand without support in Caerphilly: one very clear expression of how many felt about the all-Welsh rule was a spontaneous strike by local bus drivers who refused to take people to the Eisteddfod field.

During the coming years, Ness continued to speak out on the Welsh language. He expressed his concern that Welsh medium schools could create a Welsh speaking elite and he was worried by the disproportionately large number of Welsh speakers being recruited by the BBC in Wales. Ness's attention, however, still continued to focus on the Eisteddfod's all-Welsh rule and, as he saw it, the growing divide between Welsh and non-Welsh speakers. In 1966, for example, Leo Abse, the Labour MP for Pontypool, and Ness put down an Early Day Motion in the House of Commons on the all-Welsh rule. It was headed 'Dialogue between Welsh and non-Welsh speaking Welshmen':

> *That this House, believing that the cultural future of Wales demands the participation of English-speaking Welshmen and the end of their exclusion as the majority of the Welsh nation from important national events such as the Eisteddfod, welcomes the reproach made at the National Eisteddfod in the presidential address of Aneurin Tulfen [sic] Davies to those possessed of ghetto attitudes; and approves his call for a dialogue between the non-Welsh speaking and the Welsh-speaking at the National Eisteddfod believing that such a dialogue could lead to a re-vitalising of the cultural and intellectual life of Wales and Monmouthshire.*

Two years later Ness Edwards and Leo Abse again took the lead in expressing concerns about the Welsh language. In 1967 Professor Charles Gittins published his report on Primary Education in Wales. Much of the report concentrated on how the Welsh language could be protected and promoted through Primary School education. A reservation was, however, entered by a Welsh-speaking academic who questioned whether it was appropriate to give the Welsh language such a prominent position in Primary education.

Ness and Leo Abse were not slow in picking up the significance of this reservation and in February 1968 they, and four other Welsh MPs, wrote a strong letter to the Secretary of State at the Department of Education and Science. The reservation by Professor Marsh was, they wrote, "a timely note of warning". The six MPs gave notice that they would "oppose" attempts to enforce bilingualism in Welsh Primary Schools, believing that there ought to be parental choice in accordance with the 1944 Education Act. Furthermore, the MPs made it clear that if any extra finance were to be available the "first priority" should be the improvement of school buildings, the extension of nursery education and better provision for children with learning difficulties, rather than the Welsh language.

If Ness had reservations about the role of the Welsh language in Welsh society, he was an implacable opponent of all moves to give institutional expression to Welsh identity. Ness saw Welsh nationalism as a negative and dangerous creed. As such, he believed that it had to be opposed and resisted at all times; bending to nationalist pressure would never work as a political tactic because every "concession" to the nationalists, far from satisfying their demands, would, he believed, merely encourage them to press for more. The only way forward was on the basis of unity between working people in all parts of the United Kingdom. This was one of Ness's central beliefs throughout his entire political career and it led him to become one of the great 'hate figures' of Welsh nationalism.

1948 saw the first moves towards Wales being recognised as a political entity. In that year the Labour Government established 'The Council for Wales and Monmouthshire' and although the Council was only a nominated and an advisory body to central government, mainly on economic issues, it did mean that there was now a focus for Welsh interests within Wales. Under the chairmanship of the North Wales trade union leader, Huw T. Edwards, the 27 member Council drew its membership from industry, agriculture, local authorities, education and other Welsh interests. In its terms of reference it was to meet from time to time, and at least quarterly, for the interchange of views and information on developments and trends in the economic and cultural fields in Wales and Monmouthshire. In addition, the Council was to provide information to the Government so that it was "adequately informed" of the impact of Government policies on the Principality. Although the Council had no powers, through its recommendations on the structure of Government in Wales, it kept the issue of devolution on the political agenda for most of the 1950s.

The main vehicle for those who favoured 'Home Rule' was, at this time, the cross-Party Parliament for Wales Campaign. Supported strongly by activists from the Liberal Party, the Communist Party and Plaid Cymru, the Campaign was cold-shouldered by the Labour Party in Wales*. However, a number of Welsh Labour MPs, particularly those recently elected for rural seats in north west and west Wales, were quietly supportive of the Campaign and S. O. Davies, the left wing and maverick MP for Merthyr, openly gave it his backing.

In 1954 S.O. Davies was fortunate in having his name drawn in the House of Commons ballot to bring forward a Private Member's Bill. The Bill S.O. drew up was on the subject of the "Better Governance of Wales" and it proposed a

*Although the Bargoed Labour Party Ward sent delegates to one of its Conferences in May 1954.

Legislative Welsh Parliament or Senate. It had its Second Reading in the House on 4 March 1955.

The debate in the Commons saw a sparsely attended Chamber but a packed public gallery. As was expected, Ness presented a powerful case against the Bill. He quoted undeniable figures to demonstrate that, if S.O.'s "separatism" was ever to come about miners' wages would plummet, the education system would be impoverished, the railways would descend into chaos and local government would go bankrupt. To Ness it seemed that "the student advocates" of a Welsh Parliament lived by the slogan "Hate the English, but take their money".

Predictably, the Bill failed to get its Second Reading by 48 votes to 14. The Bill's supporters had been delivered a huge body-blow and had lost the argument, not least to Ness Edwards through his powerful marshalling of cold, hard facts and figures. Saunders Lewis, the former Leader of Plaid Cymru, penned the following verse in response to the Home Rulers' defeat; words which say more about Saunders Lewis than those he attacked:

> *There's nice it would be by petition*
> *or the luck of S.O. in the draw*
> *Without sending people to prison*
> *or drowning the nation in gore*
> *But to get with smooth vote-catching faces*
> *a Parliament in Cathays Park*
> *'Twould be just like the Temple of Peace is,*
> *where the modern Welsh rabble could nark*
> *A beggarly polyglot farce*
> *for Nobody, Ness and Nye's arse.*

Although the Parliament for Wales Campaign soon collapsed, the debate over the National Question continued inside the Labour Party and the Welsh Group of the PLP. Ness was now determined to make the running in the argument and in 1956 published a pamphlet entitled *'Is This the Road?'* In moderate but extremely effective prose, Ness began by arguing that Social Democracy must be judged not only by advances in "material standards", whether it is the number owning cars or television sets, or the general standard of living. It was also important to take into account the role the citizens play in the community. In a developing Social Democracy, Ness argued, there ought to be "fundamental tests" to ensure that the citizen has a bigger say in, and more power and central control over, the life of his community. Social Democracy was as much about increasing the significance of the individual as it was about raising the standard of life.

Democracy, then, had to be experienced regularly in every day life if it was to impact upon the lives of ordinary people. More than that, democracy could only be effective if it was strong on the ground, in the locality. "The more power is centralised, the more democracy is weakened; the more power resides in the localities, the stronger is democracy at its roots". Ness believed that "as power is centralised, local democracy becomes atrophied". This trend towards over-centralisation meant that "paperwork" was counting more than people. The Executives, who were increasingly running people's lives, were living in "paper towers", out of touch with humanity "ungettable, untouchable, and unaccountable".

Ness acknowledged that there was a wider debate taking place in the Labour Party about the future extent of public ownership and, later in the pamphlet, he explained why "full accountability to the elected representatives of the people ought to be the first principle of public ownership". The main message of the pamphlet, however, emphasised in bold print, was that the trend towards centralisation in society and industry was causing more and more people to lose significance in their locality. Thus "certain movements" were being given impetus in Wales and Scotland. People were beginning to believe that if they returned to the past then there would be "significance" once again in the life of the community. Such views, stated Ness, were most prevalent among the "so-called intellectuals". Ultimately, nationalism, devolution and federalism were all forms of a protest "against the political vacua of their lives".

Ness did concede that such people at least had a vision and it was better to have a debate on these issues rather than have "dull apathy". Nevertheless, Ness did not hold back in his condemnation of nationalism:

> ... the creation of new boundaries and new separations is no solution to the problem of the political vacuum that lies at the base of our social structure. You don't give greater social significance to the citizens by changing his or her national title.

For Ness it was perverse to "cut the UK into small parts" when the nations of Europe were finding that they were too small to develop their own atomic energy programme. Instead, Ness argued, that what was needed in England, Scotland and Wales was transference of power to the people, "an enrichment of local democratic authority".

In Wales this would require reversing the growing trend towards appointing unelected people to public bodies. Ness alluded to the fact that thousands of individuals were engaged in a "rash of committees" dealing with a range of activities, without any co-ordination and with no overall purpose. In an appendix to the pamphlet Ness provided a list of all the bodies in Wales which were appointed. The list included bodies concerned with industry, education, agriculture, land pests, civil aviation, ancient monuments, transport, forestry and much else. Too much government was being done for the people and too little by the people; too much was being done by individuals appointed by Whitehall and too little by people elected by the citizens of Wales.

If Wales was to be democratised the "intellectuals of Wales should stop chasing butterflies" and, instead, focus on practical changes. As a first step Ness proposed a radical change in the nature of the Council for Wales. In place of Ministerial appointments, Ness suggested that the Council for Wales should consist of representatives nominated by each County and Borough Council in Wales. There should be 100 such representatives, already with an electoral mandate from the people, drawn from all parts of Wales with each representing approximately 300,000 people.

This re-vamped Council for Wales would then take over the functions of the growing number of advisory bodies in Wales. The membership of these committees, proposed Ness, should, in the main, be drawn from the membership of the Council. When there would be a need to bring in expertise, Ness thought that this should happen, so long as a democratic majority was always maintained on each committee. These advisory bodies, in effect, would become part of the Council for Wales, reporting to the Departments of Government which set them up, but also reporting to the full Council, which would determine their composition.

Ness believed that the relationship between the Council and Central Government could not be static. He thought that once the Council for Wales's role had been expanded in the way he described, its advisory powers should continue to grow. Going beyond the democratisation of these structures which already existed, Ness argued that the Council should be a more general advisory body to Central Government on "what would be desirable in Wales" on a whole range of different issues. Such a Council, with its committees covering virtually every aspect of Government, would, said Ness, "provide a new democratic method of citizen participation". A similar structure could, in Ness's view, also be introduced in Scotland and each of the English regions. Wales, however, had the opportunity to "blaze the trail".

But Ness refused to see the issue of democracy and accountability in a departmentalised way. Ness always had a holistic vision of both the United Kingdom and Britain's society and economy. That is why, in the pamphlet, Ness went on to touch upon issues he hoped, at a later date, to expand upon. As Ness thought that nationalisation would inevitably be extended, he saw the main issue of what he called "citizen control" becoming ever more pressing. Instead of creating a healthy democratic society, Ness saw the danger of there being a "managerial revolution rule by the managers and acquiescence by the people". And when there was acquiescence this would lead to apathy and that, in turn, would mean that the citizen had no rights. To address this democratic deficit, Ness believed there was a need to re-organise Parliament and he promised to consider the issue in a different context.

In addition, there was also a need to democratise how the nationalised industries and services were themselves run. Here Ness gave the example of the Health Service. He described how, what he called "downwards democratic control" was completely absent from the Health Service because all positions in the Service were ministerially appointed. This was in stark contrast to how things were run when there were "old local authority hospitals". Instead of those who were dependent on Ministerial patronage or civil servants, running much of the Health Service, Ness favoured the local authorities playing a key role. He also wanted to see local authorities being central to the organisation of "electricity distribution". As a rule of thumb, Ness believed that "where ever power can be taken from the hands of nominated people and placed in the hands of elected people, democracy is strengthened and the citizen is given more control".

However, as with Parliamentary scrutiny, much more thought needed to be given as to how nationalised industries and services should be run in the future. Ness gave a big hint that more ideas were to be forthcoming. There could be no denying the importance of this agenda; only by addressing these issues could there be any hope of ending the "political anaemia" which was sweeping across the country.

Welsh devolution, said Ness, had to be viewed in this broader democratic context. What was needed in Wales, as in the rest of the UK, was for the people to go forward to new forms of democracy, rather than back to old forms. Democracy had to be "rooted in the localities" and made an every day experience of the citizen in Wales and elsewhere. There should be nothing less than "a crusade" to bring power back to the people. The citizen must be much more than a mere number on a file; the individual in a modern state had to be the embodiment of the principles of accountability and democracy.

With the publication of his pamphlet in March 1956, Ness made a concerted effort to raise the profile of the issues in its pages. His ideas for expanding the role of the Council for Wales became known as the 'Caerphilly Doctrine' and attracted supportive and critical attention in Wales and beyond. In the pro-Labour *Daily Herald* and in the *News Chronicle*, Ness wrote articles taking forward the main proposal of the pamphlet, the expanded role of the Council for Wales. In the *News Chronicle*, Ness wrote that in the "patternless jungle" of appointed committees in Wales there had arisen a "miasma of ideas". Without naming the Welsh nationalists or any of his Labour colleagues, he poured scorn on those who worshipped tradition and, instead, urged people to look to the future and embrace democracy.

Ness gave a number of radio and television interviews in Wales explaining his case and most of the Welsh press gave his pamphlet quite detailed coverage. The *Daily Post*, with a wide circulation in North Wales, was especially positive in its reportage, describing Ness's pamphlet as "a stimulating document". Acknowledging Ness as "an important figure in the Labour Party", the paper believed that Ness had many significant things to say and that he had expressed himself in a "forthright manner". The newspaper agreed with Ness's view that there was a lamentable lack of popular participation, or even interest in, local and national decision making and, without passing judgement, it gave a fair and objective summary of Ness's proposals.

The *Western Mail* also gave the pamphlet extensive coverage. Its correspondent, after making some flippant remarks about the political complexion of the Welsh Labour Group, described Ness's pamphlet as "blunt", displaying "surprising candour" in its analysis of the way the nationalised industries were run. Unfortunately, the newspaper failed to understand the essence of Ness's political approach, seeing the pamphlet as an attempt "to see what can be saved" from "the prison of State despotism". On the proposals for the Council of Wales, the correspondent had some sympathy with Ness's arguments but concluded by attacking Ness for still being committed to nationalisation.

Two other commentators in print were critical of the pamphlet. In the *News Chronicle*, one commentator wrote in the 'Cornel y Cymro' column, that while it was unanswerable that there was insufficient public involvement in decision making, there had to be a serious doubt about Ness's key proposal. Was there not a danger, wrote the columnist, that the re-vamped Council for Wales would be a glorified County Council? Then, a few months later, a 'special correspondent' in the *Cymric Democrat*, made a more thorough criticism of Ness's pamphlet. In terms of its political impact, the correspondent thought that the "stones" Ness was throwing from Caerphilly Castle would have varying degrees of accuracy: some would be wide of their mark ("much maligned civil servants"), while others would hit their target ("some highly placed comrades"). So far as the arguments were concerned, the correspondent doubted whether the nationalised industries were as undemocratic as Ness suggested and he questioned whether Aneurin Bevan would be in favour of taking the Health Service "outside of politics". On the subject of the Council for Wales, the commentator was not impressed with the suggestion that local councillors should have more influence. This was because of a supposed lack of "suitable personnel". Nor did he believe that Ness had given sufficient thought to the status which the terms 'elected' and 'unelected' conferred on a body. By this the correspondent meant that if the Council for Wales was to be made up of elected members (albeit indirectly elected), there was a case for it to have "executive" rather than merely advisory powers.

Back in the Welsh Group of the PLP in Westminster, the arguments would soon be raging. The Welsh table in the Commons Tearoom was to be the centre of heated discussion. To say that there were two camps of Welsh Labour MPs would be over-simplistic, but it was the case that there were two 'poles' in the debate that was to follow. On one side of the argument was James Griffiths, who was given Frontbench responsibility for Welsh affairs in 1956, Lady Megan Lloyd George, MP for Carmarthen until her death in 1966, Goronwy Roberts, MP for Caernarvon, and a number of the newer MPs, drawn from professional backgrounds and mainly representing rural seats in the west and north west of Wales. At the other 'pole' were Ness Edwards and Aneurin Bevan, and a number of other Valleys MPs, nearly all of whom came from working class and, usually, mining backgrounds.

The debate in the Welsh Group was not so much a debate about whether Labour should favour 'devolution' as such - nearly everyone accepted that it was desirable to bring power closer to the people - the real issue was whether Labour should develop constitutional arrangements which explicitly recognised Wales 'as a nation'. To make progress and to work to a common position on devolution and other issues, the Welsh Group had agreed as far back as November 1952 to establish five panels, one of which was a Machinery of Government Working Group. This Working Group was to look at local government, devolution, the Council for Wales and other related issues. Initially it had a membership consisting of Aneurin Bevan, Jim Griffiths, Cledwyn Hughes, MP for Anglesey, and Ness Edwards. Ness appears to have assumed the chairmanship of the Group early on. In the period after its formation the panel seems to have met only spasmodically. However, in April 1953 it recommended to the Welsh Group as a whole that it should press for two full days for debates on Welsh affairs on the floor of the House in each Parliament and that there should be a "regional breakdown" of Government estimates and statistical information. This was agreed by the Group but with S. O. Davies and D. R. Grenfell, MP for Gower, objecting to the term 'regional'. 1956 however saw the group working in earnest. Still under the chairmanship of Ness, who was promoting his own ideas in '*Is This the Road?*', the working group agreed to consider a number of papers put forward by Goronwy Roberts. By March 1957 these papers had been refined down to a single memorandum. At the heart of the Roberts paper was a proposal to create a Secretary of State for Wales, with powers in line with the proposals made by the Council for Wales. Responsibility for four Government Departments Health, Education, Agriculture and Forestry, and Housing and Local Government were to be transferred to a new Welsh Office.

Ness argued strongly against the Roberts paper. In very full Minutes of the key meeting of the Machinery of Government Panel on 26 March 1957 it is recorded how Ness had stated "that dissatisfaction with the present arrangements [of Government] stemmed from a wider basis than a national one," and he did not think that it was particularly a Welsh problem; it was political and not national.

The Minutes went on to record how Ness argued that the Panel should look for a United Kingdom solution and that Ness "was not convinced that there was any greater case for a Secretary of State for Wales than there was for a Secretary of State for, say, Yorkshire or Lancashire. He did not subscribe to the view held by some people that Wales was a separate nation".

Goronwy Roberts responded to Ness by saying that "if it was true that the problem should be looked from a functional angle, then everything the Labour Government did with regard to the setting up of the Council for Wales was wrong". He argued that the appointment of a Secretary of State for Wales was a "reasonable, practicable reform which could be conducted within the framework of the UK". When the proposal for a Secretary of State for Wales was put to the vote of the Panel of Members it was carried by six votes to two. Ness and, presumably, Arthur Probert, MP for Aberdare, being the two dissidents.

The next battlefield was the wider Labour Party. In 1957 a 'special committee' was established by the Party consisting of representatives of the National Executive Committee, the Parliamentary Labour Party, the Welsh Group of the PLP and the Welsh Council of Labour. At first the meetings were chaired by Walter Padley, MP for Ogmore, and then Jim Griffiths, but the later and more crucial meetings were chaired by the Leader of the Labour Party, Hugh Gaitskell. The committee's brief was to examine the proposals for a Secretary of State for Wales and the creation of a Welsh Office.

At the very first meeting of the group, Ness Edwards introduced the recommendations of the Welsh Group's Panel by explaining that whilst the recommendations were approved by a majority of the Panel, his own position was "an extremely reserved one". This was something of an understatement as he went on to tell the committee that he was "fundamentally opposed" to the recommendations because he saw the United Kingdom as one economic unit. Under the recommendations, the Secretary of State for Wales would determine the level of spending for each devolved department and this meant, argued Ness, that Wales would, in effect, be separately administered and governed.

However, other members of the committee took a contrary view, pointing out that the proposed reforms were "reasonable". They would introduce changes in the machinery of government which were overdue and would give Wales a valuable voice at the Cabinet table. Politically, it was stated, the reforms would stop the nationalists' advance or, as it was diplomatically recorded in the Minutes, the proposals would "do untold good to the psychology at present growing in Wales". Some proponents of the recommendations went further warning that, if the Labour Party was not prepared to take "some action", then it would be "inviting" setbacks at the polls.

Later meetings of the committee, at the House of Commons, heard more arguments in favour of the proposals from Jim Griffiths, and arguments against by Aneurin Bevan, supported by Ness Edwards. Cliff Protheroe, the Secretary of the Welsh Council of Labour, recorded in his memoirs that Nye, who was now Deputy Leader of the Party, became "very emotional" but was countered by Jim Griffiths who used "all his power as a negotiator" to persuade his colleagues. It became clear that things were moving in Jim Griffiths's favour when it could be seen that he had succeeded in winning over Hugh Gaitskell. With a General Election approaching there was now the prospect of Labour going into that election with its Leader and Deputy Leader holding different views on a key policy area. The potentially embarrassing situation was resolved, however, when, in the middle of a "heated debate", Nye suddenly surprised everyone by proposing "That we include in our policy statement, that a Secretary of State for Wales will be appointed".

After this, the meeting was brought to an abrupt close as the policy of the Party was effectively settled. On leaving the meeting, Cliff Protheroe recorded how he turned to Ness Edwards and expressed his surprise at what had just happened. Ness responded by saying cryptically "If you were Member of this House, Cliff, you would not be surprised at what has taken place this afternoon".

Labour's plan for devolved government came to nothing because the Party again lost the General Election of 1959. Ness, however, saw an opportunity for pursuing his goal of increasing governmental accountability and in March 1960 he successfully persuaded the House of Commons Select Committee on Procedures and the Conservative Minister for Welsh Affairs to adopt his idea of a Welsh Grand Committee. This was a significant success for the Labour Party. Although Ness was disappointed that the Committee never reached his expectations - in later years he likened it to a "Sunday School Anniversary" - at the time the Welsh Grand was an important innovation, providing a distinct and regular forum at Westminster for Welsh issues. It did nothing though to dampen the enthusiasm of some of Ness's colleagues who wanted a stronger commitment to Welsh devolution from the Party.

Much to the chagrin of Ness, in 1961 Hugh Gaitskell, under pressure from Jim Griffiths, reaffirmed Labour's commitment to the creation of a Secretary of State for Wales and a Welsh Office and when Harold Wilson became Leader he, too, made it clear that a Labour Government would honour this pledge. Indeed, after Labour won the 1964 General Election, the post of Secretary of State was established with a Welsh Office in Cardiff. James Griffiths was appointed the first Secretary of State for Wales in 1964, to be succeeded by Cledwyn Hughes in 1966.

If these years saw huge changes in the government machinery in Wales, they also witnessed the dramatic emergence of Plaid Cymru as a significant political force. In July 1966, Gwynfor Evans defeated Labour's Gwilym Prys Davies in the

Carmarthen by-election and became Plaid's first ever Member of Parliament. Then, in March 1967, Plaid came within 2,306 votes of capturing Rhondda West in Labour's coalfield heartland. The shockwaves of these two results hit the Labour Party hard. The response of Cledwyn Hughes was to press for more devolution, but now in the context of local government reform. The Welsh Council of Labour had formally agreed at its conference in 1966 to support an 'elected' Regional Council and with Emrys Jones having succeeded Cliff Protheroe as Regional Secretary, there was now a more sympathetic ear to pro-devolution arguments in the Party's Welsh headquarters.

A totally different response to the rise of the Welsh nationalists came from Ness Edwards. He believed that the government had been totally wrong in its approach to the growing "problem" of nationalism. Rather than making concessions to the nationalists' demands, Ness argued that the government ought to adopt an alternative approach based on extending "accountability" and bringing about a genuine devolution of power which transcended national boundaries.

In the early part of 1967, 19 Welsh Labour MPs signed a confidential letter to Cledwyn Hughes and Harold Wilson stating their opposition to an elected Council for Wales. Ness Edwards was almost certainly the person behind the letter and Richard Crossman, the Leader of the House and the Chairman of the Cabinet's Home Affairs Committee, recorded accurately in his diary that the proposal for an elected Welsh Council was opposed by most of the South Wales MPs "such as Ness Edwards, since the miners don't in the least want a Welsh Parliament and think any surrender to the nationalists is an act of cowardly appeasement". Soon after Dick Crossman made this entry in his diary, Ness, wrote to Crossman urging that the Government should not now come down in favour of an "appointed Welsh Council". In Ness's view, at this stage, an appointed body would be a step towards the ultimate goal of the pro-devolutionists who Ness called the "silly boys". To date, the majority of Welsh Labour MPs had "acquiesced" to the steps "initiated by Jim Griffiths and now being followed up by Cledwyn". Probably realising that the Cabinet had already rejected the idea of an 'elected' Council, Ness told Crossman that now was the time to be "positive" rather than "negative".

The positive approach to which Ness referred was the idea of a 'Select Committee on Welsh Administration'. Ness proposed a committee of about twelve Members drawn from Welsh constituencies to ensure "accountability" of the Executive "in relation to Regional machinery". This would replicate what was already happening with other Select Committees and Government Departments. Unlike any body sitting in Cardiff, the Select Committee would be part of the "structure of Parliament" and would not, therefore, be a forum "for the Tories or the Nats". Politically, Ness was confident that such a Select Committee "would effectively deal with the drive to separatism that is behind the agitation of those who are nationalists first and Socialists second".

At the end of 1967 and in the early months of 1968, Ness's idea was earnestly discussed by the Welsh Labour Group of MPs. In January, a 'Memorandum' was drawn up by Ness setting out the "consensus" of the Group. Essentially, the Group was of the opinion that a new Select Committee should be established as Ness proposed. It should "investigate the functioning of the administration throughout the Principality" and prepare reports for debate in the Welsh Grand Committee and on Welsh Day on the floor of the House. Most of the Members should be drawn from Welsh constituencies but, because the committee would consider revenue issues, which were not solely Welsh matters, the membership, the Group argued, should not be exclusive to Welsh Members.

Ness's proposal was well received across the Group, with strong support coming from younger Members such as Ted Rowlands, MP for Cardiff North, and Donald Anderson, MP for Monmouth. Before long Ness began to talk about his idea in a somewhat different way. No longer did he hope that the Select Committee would be concerned only with the Welsh Office but Ness came to see it having "powers of supervision and enquiry" over every Government Department which impacted upon Wales. The *Western Mail*'s, Chief Political Correspondent, perhaps stated the obvious when he wrote that Ness's proposal would not find any favour with those who wanted a Welsh Parliament, but he did accept that it was an "artful alternative" to Home Rule.

Despite the widespread support for Ness's proposal from Welsh Labour Members, Dick Crossman did not give a sufficiently positive response for the proposal to be implemented. In February 1968 he wrote to Ness to explain that although he had "some sympathy" with the idea of a Welsh Select Committee, he saw little chance of the "early appointment" of such a Committee because the Select Committees which had already been established meant there were difficulties in finding sufficient Members to sit on Standing Committees. The Prime Minister responded to a letter from Ness saying little more than he found Ness's idea "interesting". These somewhat lame responses meant that it was to be 11 years before progress was made on Ness's proposal. When Parliament did create a 'Welsh Affairs Select Committee' in 1979 it was based essentially on what Ness had proposed over a decade earlier.

For Ness, the struggle against the advance of political and cultural nationalism had to take place at a local level as well as in Parliament. In the late 1950s and early 1960s Ness, like many other Labour Party members in South Wales, was extremely concerned at what was seen as a concerted attempt by a Welsh speaking middle class elite to change the nature of Welsh society and politics to their advantage and to the disadvantage of the monoglot English speaking majority. The formation of Cymdeithas yr Iaith Gymraeg (the Welsh Language Society) in 1962 gave a focus for Ness's concerns.

A clear example of what Ness feared was seen in Caerphilly in January 1966 when the Labour controlled Caerphilly UDC decided to change formally the spelling of the town's name from Caerphilly to the Welsh 'Caerffili'. Ness explained to the Executive Committee of the Caerphilly Divisional Party that there was a "danger of the action being interpreted as a concession to those elements in the Welsh establishment who were working to impose a language bar to the advancement of non-Welsh speaking people in the field of public employment". One of the councillors who had voted for the change stated that he had done so because he did not see it as a matter of "outstanding importance". The majority of the Executive members, however, saw things differently and a resolution was passed congratulating Ness on the stand he had taken.

The EC also agreed to pursue the matter with the Labour Group on the Council and a member of the Executive was deputed to meet the councillors. A month later it was reported back to the EC that the majority of the Labour Group now favoured "Caerphilly". The proposed change was quietly dropped.

The discussions at these Labour Party meetings brought to the fore a number of Ness's concerns about the Welsh language. The "discrimination" against monoglot English speakers in public appointments which Ness feared, could, he believed, have a number of adverse consequences. As well as being wrong in itself, it could lead to second-rate administrations with Local Authorities being run in the interests of a minority of the population. This was why the "infiltration" of local government by Welsh nationalists had to be stopped.

As we have seen, throughout his years in Parliament Ness vigorously opposed Welsh nationalism and consistently argued for a different approach to the 'Welsh Question' to that advanced by James Griffiths and Cledwyn Hughes. Ness always took the view that concessions would only serve to whet the appetite of those who wanted nothing less than the separation of Wales from England. Often Ness's arguments seemed to fall on deaf ears within the leadership but, in April 1968, a few weeks before Ness died, Harold Wilson demoted Cledwyn Hughes by moving him from the position of Secretary of State for Wales to be Minister of Agriculture. His replacement was the strongly anti-nationalist, anti-devolutionist, MP for Cardiff West, George Thomas. Harold Wilson had concluded that there was a need for a change of approach in Wales. He now believed that a firm stand had to be taken against the Welsh nationalists, mirroring what the Scottish Secretary had done north of the border. Perhaps Ness Edwards had, after all, more influence than most commentators realised.

CHAPTER 6

ELDER STATESMAN

Free of his Frontbench responsibilities from 1960, Ness now focussed his energies on those issues he felt passionate about. Top of his list was Britain's relationship with the Common Market. In articles and speeches, in late 1961 and early 1962 especially, Ness argued that the Labour Party should end its ambivalence towards the Common Market and instead advocate Britain's membership of the "European Community".

In an article in the *Western Mail* in January 1962, for example, Ness spelt out the pro-European argument in no uncertain terms. The case, for Ness, was essentially an economic one. Britain had a highly developed economy and it needed access to a larger market on its doorstep. Just as a village cannot support a super-market, wrote Ness, a single country, like Britain "is entirely inadequate" to provide a consumer base for the country's industrial products.

The choice for the British people was clear: either to become part of a vibrant European Community or "become an offshore island off the coast of the European mainland" with a struggling economy propped up with illusions of "imperial grandeur". While Ness was happy to concede that for economic reasons the decision whether to join the Common Market was not an easy one, he dismissed out of hand the arguments of those who were concerned about supposed national sovereignty. Some of the arguments, thought Ness, amounted to wanting to remain a big fish in a small pond, "even though the pool is drying up".

And taking advantage of his new 'freedom' on the backbenches, Ness took a swipe at the anti-Europeans of both the left and right of the Labour Party. Ness thought it "beyond belief" that those of the "so-called left", who had opposed unilateral intervention in Suez, should now claim the "absolute right of isolated action". Equally, he lashed-out at the right in the Party, including the Leader, Hugh Gaitskell, who defended Britain's membership of NATO but was antagonistic to the Common Market. To such colleagues Ness asked if they realised that Britain's ability to be effective militarily depended on the country's economic strength.

In early 1962 Ness's European commitment was strengthened still further when he visited Franco's Spain with four other Labour MPs. During his visit he met workers' leaders (trade unions being banned) and attended the first Congresso Syndical. He left the country impressed that the syndicate officials he met wanted change but without bloodshed and a civil war. Equally, he was clearly touched by those who begged the delegation to help them make contact with progressive opinion in the rest of Europe, so that "the ideas of democracy" could blow through the "cobwebbed windows of Spain". Given that Ness had wanted to fight for the International Brigade in Spain in the 1930s but, some say, he had been dissuaded from doing so by the Communist Party, this visit to Spain was particularly poignant for Ness.

During what turned out to be the latter years of Ness's Parliamentary career, the Member for Caerphilly intervened on a wide range of issues. As well as speaking his mind on the Common Market and keeping a watching brief on devolution, Ness spoke up in favour of nuclear energy, and was roundly condemned by the NUM as a consequence. He also continued to follow developments in television and telecommunications, making a strong submission to the Pilkington Inquiry in 1962, and he served as Chairman of the Welsh Labour Group's Panel on Radio and Television. Increasingly, too, Ness found himself being regarded as a kind of Labour Party Elder Statesman. In that unrequested role, he successfully campaigned for an improvement in MPs' pension rights so that ex-Members would no longer have to rely on discretionary awards. From time to time, Ness also found himself acting as an unofficial arbiter between the Party leadership and left wing Labour rebels. For instance, in March 1961, Ness wrote to Hugh Gaitskell asking for the Party Whip to be restored to Michael Foot, MP for Ebbw Vale, and four others who had broken ranks and voted against the Government's defence estimates. On this occasion, however, his conciliatory efforts were thwarted because the rebels repeated their actions and, in so doing, undermined Ness's efforts. It was, no doubt, because of this role that there was press speculation in 1967 that Ness might have been made Chairman of the PLP after Emmanuel Shinwell resigned.

At a local level, throughout his Parliamentary career Ness had been a champion of Caerphilly Castle. He recognised the Castle's historic significance but also its potential for attracting tourists and developing the town of Caerphilly as a whole. The MP for Caerphilly was especially pleased when, in the mid 1950s, Harman Nicholls MP, Parliamentary Secretary to the Ministry of Works, accepted Ness's invitation to visit Caerphilly Castle to see for himself the progress that was being made on the Castle's restoration. The Minister, accompanied by his officials, took part in detailed discussions with the local authority about a five year plan of work on the Castle. The plan included building new entrances and bridges and the restoration of the elaborate, medieval water defences - improvements which transformed the Castle's environs and its accessibility.

During the last few years of Ness's life two other issues which were close to his heart received much of his time and attention. The first was the economic future of the Rhymney Valley, his own Parliamentary Constituency, and linked to it, the decline of the coal industry.

In the days of the 1945-51 Labour Government the face of South Wales had began to change for the better. Public ownership of the mines had brought job security and higher wages and new industrial estates had begun to create at least some economic diversification. But by the late 1950s the post-war optimism was evaporating as recession led to a significant increase in Welsh unemployment. The South Wales Valleys, including the Rhymney Valley, were hit hard with the coal industry facing the beginning of what was to be a process of inexorable decline. The closure of Llanbradach colliery, just north of Caerphilly, in 1961 was a particularly serious blow for Ness's Constituency.

In the face of these economic problems Ness went on the offensive. Addressing a meeting of the Bargoed Branch of the Amalgamated Engineering Union in May 1962, Ness pointed the finger of blame for what was happening in the coal industry at the National Coal Board (NCB) Chairman, Lord Robens. He was, said Ness, simply copying the policy of managers of private enterprises. The most productive and efficient parts of the industry were being developed and other parts being left to one side. The long-term consequences of such a policy, predicated Ness, would be disastrous for both the country and the industry.

Ness was at pains to explain that Lord Robens could not be blamed for closing exhausted pits or pits that technically or geologically could not be made a success. In these situations the problem was the absence of any effort by Government to provide assistance and alternative employment for the areas affected. Because of the indifference of central Government, argued Ness, Lord Robens should not be oblivious to the suffering of the community. Unless Government was prepared to shoulder its responsibility and provide alternative employment, there should be no slimming down of the coal industry.

With his in depth understanding of the coal industry, Ness realised that Robens was moving away from seeing the coal industry as one economic entity. Instead, Robens was attempting to assess profitability on a pit by pit or District by District basis. "Cut-throat competition" between the coalfields would become the order of the day with coalfields outside the Midlands and Yorkshire having a "pretty grim future". For Ness this was short-termism gone mad; in a crude monetary sense there might be short-term savings but Robens, with the approach of a "harassed shop manager", was going to make the future pay a very heavy price. The unavoidable question was "how would the country meet its energy needs once the easily mined coal had been exhausted?"

In 1958, in his New Year's message to his constituents, Ness warned that such were the economic problems facing the Valleys, there was a real danger that "the life" of the Valleys would be lost. With the coal industry contracting, the drift of industry to the coast and the wilful indifference of Government to these problems, Ness believed that it was up to the people of the Valleys themselves to seize the initiative. As Ness wrote, if the Valleys were to be saved, "we will have to find the means to save them ourselves".

Following this rallying cry, the Chairman of Gelligaer UDC convened a conference of all the local authorities in the Rhymney Valley to discuss the future of the Valley. The conference was addressed by Aneurin Bevan, Harold Finch, MP for Bedwellty, and Ness himself. The main conclusion of the conference was that there was an urgent need to encourage new industries into the Rhymney Valley and that it was hopeless to wait for Whitehall to take a lead; if anything was to be done the initiative had to come from the local authorities. In more tangible terms the conference proposed the creation of three trading, or industrial estates, one each in the southern, northern and middle parts of the Valley. This was the way, said Ness, to translate Government failure into local authority success.

In the four years after the conference, Gelligaer UDC established a trading estate at Tir-y-Berth, but faced difficulties in establishing one at the top end of the Valley. Caerphilly UDC, however, led the way with plans for a new industrial estate at Pontygwindy, on the main road leading north from Caerphilly town centre. Originally 17 acres of land had been bought by the Council some years earlier with the intention of building a new housing estate. Now this land was used to establish a "tailor-made" light industrial estate. Within two years of advertising Pontygwindy the 17 acres had been filled and an additional 23 acres were added in 1962. By 1966, 28 firms either occupied the sites or were about to move in, creating approximately 2,500 new jobs. This trading estate was unlike so many of the earlier estates in that Pontygwindy was designed to blend into the local area. Ness confidently predicted that, when completed, the estate would be as attractive as any in Britain.

Key to the success of the Pontygwindy Estate was the Labour Council's decision to reduce "red-tape". It was recognised that industrialists and potential investors could not afford to wait for long periods before they had Council decisions and it was therefore agreed to circumvent normal processes by creating a special Industrial Development Committee. This Committee, under the chairmanship of Dr. Blundell, a young and talented councillor, was given full delegate powers to take decisions without having to wait for Council's confirmation. All aspects of negotiation, with the exception of housing for essential workers, were subject to this attenuated procedure. The importance of this new approach was recognised fully by Ness.

Buoyed up by the success of the Pontygwindy venture, when British Railways announced the closure of its Locomotive Works in Van Road in 1963, with the loss of 400 jobs, many of them highly skilled, Caerphilly UDC acted quickly and decisively. Within six months of the closure of the "Welsh Swindon", the site was purchased by the local authority and all the land and buildings made available by the authority had been taken-up by firms. By March 1966 it could be said that the site housed firms who, between them, had the potential to employ over 2,000 people - double the number employed by British Railways when the Locomotive Works was in its heyday. Among the firms on the estate were J. J. Casting Investments Co. Ltd., and J. J. Casting Investments (Heat Treatment) Ltd., the Roath Furnishing Company, Procter Bros. (Wireworks Ltd.) and, perhaps most importantly of all, South Wales Switchgear Ltd., initially employing 160 workers but with a promise to take on between 400 and 500 over the next two to three years.

Given the success of these industrial estates it is hardly surprising that Harold Wilson in 1964, when he was Leader of the Opposition, willingly accepted the invitation of Ness and the local authority to have the new estate named after him. On 4 March 1966, as Prime Minister, Harold Wilson duly opened the estate. Ness's hope, as he expressed in his speech on the day, was that Caerphilly would become the fastest growing economic centre in South Wales.

While the success that Caerphilly UDC was having in attracting fresh investment gave Ness much relief and satisfaction, there was no doubt that the continuing problems faced by the coal industry were a constant source of anguish. Perhaps with the election of a Labour Government in 1964 Ness had hoped for an end to the industry's travails. If he did, he was soon to be disabused. Colliery closures continued through the latter half of the 1960s and, despite the NCB's denials that there were any plans in the offing, in 1967 the Elliott Colliery at the top of the Rhymney Valley was closed. Although employment was provided in surrounding collieries for those who wanted to transfer, the closure of the pit was a serious blow to an area which would have enormous difficulty in attracting new industry.

During these years, in Westminster Ness took a keen interest in the work of the PLP's Trade Union Group. Indeed, apart from his local concerns, this was Ness's main focus after he left the Frontbench and it was a time when the Group had enormous influence. Tam Dalyell, the former MP and Father of the House, has remarked that the Group was undoubtedly the most influential backbench Group in Westminster. When a controversial issue was on the agenda it was not unusual for as many as 80 Labour MPs, nearly a quarter of the PLP, to attend a meeting. And nor was membership open to everyone; only those who were actually 'sponsored' by a trade union could join. Throughout the 1964 and 1966 Labour Governments, the General Secretary of the TUC, George Woodcock, and an array of other senior trade union officials and Government Ministers from the Prime Minister down, were all regular attendees of the Group's meetings. Indeed, in the mid-1960s it became "the custom" for none other than the Prime Minister to address the first meeting of the Group in a new session of Parliament.

As the Minutes of the Group indicate, in 1965 especially, the Group was very concerned about the NCB's pit closures. In the previous year, in part, one suspects, because of his deep interest in the subject, Ness became the Chairman of the Group, after George Brown stood down from the post on his entry into Government. Ness also continued as Chairman of the Miners' Group of MPs, co-authoring a 'Private and Confidential' note for the Group on the 'Future of the Mining Industry' in March 1965. The note set out a number of options for how the market for coal could be improved and suggested a more pro-active Government policy towards the industry. On pit closures the note was emphatic - there should be a new "independent" Regional Planning Board to which all proposals for closure would have to be referred. If the closure of a colliery was confirmed, then the Planning Board would have to bring forward "proper social measures". On the other hand, if a colliery was to be kept open on "social grounds", the subsequent loss should be "borne by the Treasury".

It was not, however, pit closures which dominated the last couple of years of Ness's life. Rather, it was the Wilson Government's Prices and Incomes Policy and the issue of wage restraint. When Harold Wilson succeeded Hugh Gaitskell as Leader of the Labour Party in 1963, after Gaitskell's tragic death, Ness was probably pleased that it was Wilson who took over the reins. Wilson had come from the traditional 'left' of the Party and had always kept his distance from the Party's gung-ho revisionists, opposing, for example, the re-writing of Clause IV. Moreover, Wilson had a modernising agenda which appealed to Ness. As we have seen, the MP for Caerphilly had long espoused the need for 'socialist planning' as he believed that this was the only way to create a modern and prosperous economy. He also believed that it was necessary to embrace new technology and ensure that the economy was run in an accountable way by individuals committed to the success of socialised production. Wilson's embracing of "the white hot heat of technology" therefore struck a cord with Ness, as did Wilson's commitment to State planning through the new Department of Economic Affairs (DEA). Ness was especially pleased that his friend George Brown was, as expected, appointed to lead the Department with the title of 'First Secretary', in effect Deputy Prime Minister.

Central to the DEA's work was the National Plan, published in September 1965. The main objective of the Plan was an ambitious increase in national output of 25% between 1964 and 1970. Regional Planning was seen as vital and the Government created a number of Regional Economic Planning Councils in a determined effort to increase the number of jobs in the less prosperous areas. At the same time, an Industrial Reorganisation Corporation was established to encourage greater industrial efficiency.

All of this was music to Ness's ears. Not only did he fully agree with the philosophy behind the National Plan, he also concurred with its detail, especially its emphasis on national and regional planning. Building on his long association with George Brown, Ness developed a close working relationship with Brown during 1965-66, with the First Secretary and other Government Ministers regularly attending Group meetings to discuss the implementation of the National Plan and holding informal discussions with the Group's officers.

This close working relationship was not to last. From the start of the National Plan there had been the problem of the value of Sterling and the country's Balance of Payments. There was also the need to keep inflation under control and the question of how this was to be done. Initially, the Wilson Government pressed hard for the trade unions to agree voluntary wage restraint and in 1965 the Government published a White Paper on Prices and Incomes Policy and a special Board for Prices and Incomes was established. However, the Sterling crisis of 1966 led to a six month freeze on wages and prices, followed by a further six months of tight controls. At the same time a number of deflationary measures were introduced and George Brown, who had threatened to resign, was moved to the Foreign Office. The Government's brave new National Plan was in tatters and the DEA's days were numbered.

As a consequence of these traumatic developments the Government's relationship with the trade union movement and the PLP Trade Union Group came under severe strain. Then things got worse. The Government bowed to the inevitable and in November 1967 Sterling was devalued and the Government persisted with a policy of achieving wage restraint through a statutory Prices and Incomes Policy.

The 'special relationship' between the Government and trade unions was now close to breaking point and the camaraderie which characterised the Group's relationship with the 1964-66 Government gave way to frosty confrontation. With Ness in the Chair, the PLP Trade Union Group was now absolutely central to the Government's approach to economic policy. Given the numerical strength of the Group it could even be said that the very future of the Government depended on the Group's support, or at least its acquiescence. Ness was keen to avoid a "head-on collision" between the Government and the unions and, throughout 1967, worked hard to find a "middle way" between the two. At a meeting of the Group on 13 March 1968, Ness opened the discussion on the Government's new Prices and Incomes Policy. He began by reminding people that when a Prices and Incomes Policy was first introduced, George Brown had stated that it would only be in force for a period of 12 months. In spite of that, another period of legislation was introduced to run until June 1968. Now, Ness reminded his fellow MPs, the

Government wanted further legislation to be in for at least another 18 months. The position of himself and the Group was clear, he stated, while they were "not wholly opposed" to any statutory Prices and Incomes Policy, they had not accepted that there should be "penal legislation". But Ness also warned Members, and by implication the Government, that if there was the introduction of another period of Prices and Incomes Policy and the Group were to oppose it, "then it did mean that the Government would be brought down".

Harold Wilson was acutely aware of the gravity of the situation and in February 1968 he addressed the Group for no less than 45 minutes on the need for a Prices and Incomes Policy. He then answered questions for a further 45 minutes. In the following months he met with Ness and the other officers of the Group on two separate occasions in his room in the Commons. There was, however, no meeting of minds at these meetings. Ness reported back to a full meeting of the Trade Union Group saying that the deputation had stressed to the Prime Minister just how strongly the Group felt about wage restraint and that they had "emphasised" that the Government should, at least, accept the economic arguments put forward by the TUC or come to "some amicable agreement" with the TUC on wage restraint. Later that day, 26 March, Ness and the other Group officers met with Peter Shore, who was now in charge of the DEA, and Ness put to him a number of "searching questions". Ness told Peter Shore bluntly that "penal sanctions" against the trade unions could not work and that the Government "must find a solution to the whole problem that can be accepted by the TUC".

In all of these meetings Ness displayed great skill and resourcefulness. As a staunch trade unionist, Ness understood better than anyone why the unions so strongly opposed a statutory Incomes Policy, reinforced by the threat of sanctions. At the same time he also recognised the dilemma which Harold Wilson now found himself in. While it was only too easy to criticise the Government for having allowed itself to get into the situation it was in, criticism alone did not offer a way forward for the movement. It was Ness's approach to make use of the strength of the Trade Union Group to seek to find a 'compromise' which would enhance the position of the trade unions and take the Labour movement forward as one. This is what Ness sought to achieve in his discussions with the Prime Minister and Peter Shore, and he believed that the majority of the Group which he chaired was prepared to follow such an approach. It was to Ness's great disappointment that his arguments did not find favour with the Government.

A week after Ness's meeting with Peter Shore, on 2 April Ness chaired his last meeting of the Trade Union Group. The Prime Minister attended, supported by the Chancellor, Roy Jenkins, Peter Shore and Ray Gunter, the Minister for Labour, "and several other Ministers". On this occasion Harold Wilson gave only a brief opening address but he did make it clear that it was essential that there should be a Prices and Incomes Policy. If there was not, he said, then there would be "a grave danger of the economy being so weak as to necessitate a policy of strong deflation resulting in large numbers of unemployed". Harold Wilson's tough words cut little ice with the Group and, as the Group's Minutes record, the majority of MPs who spoke from the floor expressed their strong opposition to the Government's policy on wage restraint.

This meeting of the Group had been very stormy, with one newspaper reporting that Ness had "nearly come to blows with another Member". Two weeks later, during the Easter recess, Ness suffered a heart attack while in his constituency. He was rushed to the Caerphilly District Miners' Hospital. Although Ness had collapsed at the House of Commons two years earlier and had been taken to Westminster Hospital, there can be little doubt that the strains and pressures of the previous weeks had taken a heavy toll on Ness's health. From his earlier hospitalisation Ness had made a full recovery but this time, having been in hospital for over two weeks, he developed a thrombosis in one of his legs and this led to him having a fatal heart attack. He died on 3 May 1968 at the age of 71.

In reporting Ness's death, the *Daily Express* described him as a "fiery Welsh orator, one of the best the House of Commons has known". A number of friends and colleagues paid tribute to him. Three in particular reflected both the scope and character of Ness's contribution to the Trade Union and Labour Movement, the mining community and his country of Wales. Victor Yates, MP for Birmingham Ladywood, and Ness's successor as Chairman of the Trade Union Group, spoke of Ness's "excellent work" over a period of 50 years on behalf of the "working class, both in the industrial and political field". He also paid tribute to Ness's "outstanding ability" which he displayed during his three and half years as Chairman of the PLP's Trade Union Group. Glyn Williams, President of the South Wales NUM, said Ness's passing would be a great loss to the mining communities and to the miners "to which he had given distinguished service". And George Thomas, the Secretary of State for Wales, spoke eloquently for many when he said "Wales has lost a faithful servant and I have lost a great friend. Ness Edwards was one of the great Trade Union leaders in Wales. His early life played a tremendous part in shaping his determination to use Government machinery to raise the standards of his fellow men".

Given Ness's stature within the Labour movement and Welsh politics, it is perhaps surprising that there were not more public tributes paid to him. On the other hand, it is worth remembering that Ness had few friends in the Welsh media at a time when Welsh nationalism was in the ascendant. In 1966 Gwynfor Evans had won the Carmarthen by-election and in the following year Plaid had run Labour close in Rhondda West. As soon as Ness died the immediate political speculation was whether the nationalists would now achieve a break-through in Caerphilly. With Dr. Phil Williams, a young academic, brought up in Bargoed, as their candidate Plaid Cymru fought an energetic campaign with students travelling from all over

Wales to support the Blaid. As it was, Labour's Fred Evans, a local headteacher, held the seat but with a majority of only 1,874. There was a swing to Plaid Cymru of nearly 40%.

Subsequent elections showed that the 1968 by-election was Plaid's high watermark in Caerphilly. Thereafter, although Plaid Cymru made advances in local government, they failed seriously to challenge the Labour Party at any Parliamentary election and even in the first Welsh Assembly election in 1999, the nationalists were unable to capitalise on Labour's internal problems. Maybe one of the legacies of 1968 was to ensure that Labour would never take the seat or its constituents for granted.

The by-election in 1968 also had another lasting effect: it removed from collective memory, at least outside of the constituency, the impact Ness Edwards had had on public life over a period of over four decades. For years after the by-election, whenever political commentators mentioned Caerphilly it was nearly always to refer to Plaid's near victory, rather than to acknowledge in any way Ness Edwards's work as a miners' leader or Parliamentarian. Hopefully, this modest book will at least help to set the record straight and secure a recognition of Ness Edwards as one of South Wales's greatest working class leaders.

CHAPTER 7

EPILOGUE

Perhaps more than any other Welsh politician of his generation, Ness Edwards was a man of 'principle'. While a firm believer in Parliamentary democracy, Ness always adhered to key elements of the distinctive teachings which he had embraced as a young man. Through the independent working class educational movement Ness "acquired" a Marxist political perspective which made sense of the industrial society of the South Wales Valleys of which he was part: a society dominated by one industry the coal industry - and which, in the 1920s and '30s, was becoming ever more polarised between the employed and unemployed miners, and the coal owners.

To end the exploitation which Ness saw around him, he believed that the only way forward was for the capitalist 'mode of production' to be replaced by State nationalisation (public ownership). This conviction Ness shared with the vast majority of working class political activists of his day and, unlike some of his Westminster colleagues in the 1950s and '60s, Ness never wavered from his belief in the centrality of nationalisation and State planning to achieving socialism. In fact, on one occasion in the early 1960s Ness bluntly told his local Labour Party that someone could only be a socialist if they believed in nationalisation.

The difficulty which Ness came up against during the 1950s and '60s was the mounting evidence showing that nationalisation was far from being a universal panacea for Britain's economic problems. In addition, Britain was becoming an increasingly consumerist society where choice and individual freedoms were leading to a questioning of the most fundamental of socialist beliefs. Nationalisation, certainly on the Morrisonian model, was not popular with the electorate.

Ness's response to the changing times in which he lived was not to question the principle of nationalisation but to point to the lack of "accountability" of the nationalised industries and to the way individuals were feeling alienated from the decision making processes of Government. Here the influence of the quasi-syndicalist teachings of the Plebs League and the Central Labour College can be seen to have had a continuing influence. Industrial democracy and workers' control were key themes which Ness had taken up after the First World War; in his later speeches and writings Ness tried to develop these themes and adapt them to modern circumstances. This is the distinct contribution which Ness made to socialist political thought. Sadly, Ness did not sufficiently develop his ideas for them to have a real impact.

The influence of the Labour College movement can also be seen in other aspects of Ness's politics. In the 1950s especially, but also during the 1930s when challenging the scab union, Ness was highly critical of the Communist Party. His hostility was not based merely on a dislike of particular policy lines or tactics, or even because Ness favoured evolutionary rather than revolutionary change; Ness's antagonism was derived from the knowledge that the Communist Party was inherently elitist and undemocratic. Although in the early days of the British Communist Party there were syndicalist elements in its ranks, it did not take long before it became a classic Bolshevik Party with a top down 'democratic centralist' structure. Such an organisation deeply offended Ness's ideas of openness and democratic accountability. The way the Communist Party operated also called into question the freedom of the trade union movement from outside manipulation and, again contradicting the spirit of syndicalism, it denied the rank-and-file of the trade union movement an independent role in socialist change.

For Ness, the trade unions were just as important as Parliament in the struggle for socialism. From when he was the Miners' Federation Lodge Secretary at Penallta Colliery, through to his time as the Chairman of the powerful Trade Union Group in Westminster, the trade union movement was vitally important to Ness. Indeed, this was one of the essential features of Ness's politics. Reflecting both the teaching of the Labour College Movement and the reality of South Wales before the Second World War, Ness saw the trade unions in general and the SWMF in particular as providing the bedrock of his politics.

This was the strength of Ness's politics; and yet it was also its weakness. When the South Wales Valleys were one industry, one union communities, Ness's political views had an obvious resonance. However, with the coal industry contracting in the 1950s and '60s and Valley communities becoming less homogeneous, and British society generally now more disparate, Ness's politics seemed to be less in tune with the rapidly changing world. Ness was always prepared to engage with new ideas but only if they did not contradict the central tenets of his beliefs.

Equally fascinating is the way Ness looked at the 'Welsh Question'. From an early age Ness embraced internationalism and rejected the suffocating parochialism of the Welsh nationalists. For Ness, socialism was about breaking down national barriers not building them. Because of his unflinching opposition to Welsh nationalism Ness continually drew the opprobrium of Plaid Cymru. It is interesting that the late Phil Williams, Vice President of Plaid Cymru and the Party's candidate in the Caerphilly by-election of 1968, criticised Ness (and Aneurin Bevan) in his last pamphlet, which was published posthumously. In Dr. Williams's view both Ness Edwards and Aneurin Bevan were wrong for having made the fairly obvious statement that miners in South Wales had more in common with miners in Durham than with farmers in North Wales.

Ness's opposition to Welsh nationalism was maximalist and pursued consistently. It is difficult to avoid the conclusion, however, that Ness's intense dislike of Welsh nationalism meant that he sometimes did not take on board wider considerations. His opposition to the creation of a Secretary of State for Wales is a case in point. Even though Scotland had had a Secretary of State since 1926, and much of the objective evidence suggested that Wales could only benefit from having a specific voice at the Cabinet table, Ness maintained his opposition right to the end. Similarly, Ness's strongly expressed views on the Welsh language sometimes wrongly gave the impression that he was hostile to the language, rather than being worried about the position of the overwhelming majority of Welsh people who spoke only English.

But, to be fair, Ness did recognise that the devolution agenda being pursued by leading Welsh Labour MPs, like Jim Griffiths and Cledwyn Hughes, was an incremental one, even if they seldom said so publicly. For them the creation of a Secretary of State for Wales was not an end in itself, merely a step towards a directly elected Welsh Council or Assembly. Ness thought that if this was the objective, it ought to be made clear. For Ness, such an undisclosed agenda had worrying implications. If during the 1950s and '60s devolution had been thought of more in 'democratic' than 'nationalist' terms, and more in terms of accountability rather than expediency, it is possible that Ness's attitude may have been somewhat different.

It is important to acknowledge that in some ways Ness's thinking on devolution was ahead of its time. In his pamphlet *'Is This the Road?'* Ness provided a powerful critique of the developing quango state and foreshadowed the 1997 devolution theme of 'democratisation' by over 50 years. Ness believed the answer to remote and undemocratic decision making was to transform the already existing Council for Wales into an indirectly elected body with wider responsibilities; the answer in 1997 was, of course, to have a directly elected Assembly with secondary legislative powers.

Ness also recognised that Wales needed to have distinct forums at Westminster where Welsh issues could be addressed and scrutinised. Today's Welsh Grand Committee came about because of Ness's initiative and the Welsh Affairs Select Committee was first proposed by the Member for Caerphilly.

The high point of Ness's Parliamentary career was when he was appointed Postmaster General in 1950. With some justification Ness was disappointed not to have been given a Cabinet position, not least because he had been a very effective Junior Minister at the Ministry of Labour, successfully helping to deal with the difficult post war labour situation, and had been made a Privy Counsellor in recognition of his work. But as Postmaster General, in a short space of time Ness grappled with a number of hugely complex issues ranging from the need to modernise the Post Office's industrial relations to the widespread introduction of television. Although Ness worked hard at his brief, and had a mastery of the details of the Post Office and telecommunications, he did not really give of his best at the Despatch Box. If Labour had won the 1951 General Election and Ness had continued as Postmaster General, it is more than likely that he would have been regarded as one of the 'great' Postmaster Generals.

As it was, Labour lost the Election in 1951 and did not win power again until 1964. For much of that long period Ness remained on Labour's Frontbench but by the end of the 1950s he had become increasingly dispirited because of the direction in which the Labour Party was being taken by the leadership. From 1960 until his death, Ness focussed on a range of issues which reflected his broad interests and extensive knowledge. His commitment to the trade union movement especially loomed large in these years, with his continuing opposition to the NCB's pit closure programme and his efforts to keep the Party and the trade unions together during the period of wage restraint under Harold Wilson. These years also gave Ness more opportunity to concentrate on his constituency. Unlike a number of his contemporaries, particularly those with a professional background, Ness lived in his constituency of Caerphilly and worked hard on behalf of his constituents. Having moved to the Rhymney Valley in 1927, Ness passed away in a local hospital which, appropriately, was largely paid for by the miners of the area.

Looking back at Ness's life as a whole, it is difficult to avoid the conclusion that the true historical significance of the man derives from his achievements in the earlier part of his life. The five books Ness wrote between 1924 and 1938 are quite remarkable; his books on the Workers' Theatre, Chartism and the history of the Industrial Revolution in South Wales are, in their different ways, path breaking, and his two books on the history of the Fed are fine histories by any standard, written many years before Labour History became fashionable. But it is Ness's work in rebuilding the SWMF after the 1926 General Strike and lock-out and his successful efforts in defeating the scab union in the 1930s for which Ness ought to be principally remembered.

Today, when there is only one deep mine left in South Wales, it is not easy to appreciate the importance which the Fed had for the people of the South Wales Valleys. The Fed was an effective trade union but it was much more than that. When coal mining dominated the lives of hundreds of thousands of people, the Fed became the tangible, collective expression of an entire working class community. For it to be so directly challenged, as it was in the aftermath of 1926, meant nothing less than an attack upon the entire mining community of the South Wales Valleys.

The fight against the scab union was harsh and brutal. Throughout most of the 1930s, the Fed was engaged in an intense struggle and only achieved victory after unprecedented conflicts at Taff-Merthyr and Bedwas. It was not until 1938 that it could be said that the South Wales miners had finally regained their unity of purpose and self-respect. Many people helped to achieve this historic victory but no one did more than Ness Edwards. It is not too much to say that the people of the South Wales Valleys would not today hold so strongly their Labour values if it were not for the courage, dedication and organising ability of Ness Edwards. Long may he be remembered.

NOTE ON SOURCES

Following and learning about Ness Edwards's life has been a unique journey. Ness's personal papers are held mostly by Ness's daughter, Baroness Llin Golding, and if I had not had access to them this book would have been a hollow shell. Other members of the family have been kind enough to lend me various papers and photographs and have given me the benefit of their recollections.

Additional sources of important information have been the various personal papers, lodge records and Labour Party records held in the South Wales Coalfield Collection of Swansea University; the very full Minutes of the Welsh Group of the Parliamentary Labour Party, held in the offices of the PLP in Westminster, which, unlike today's Group Minutes, often provide verbatim accounts of controversial debates and, to my surprise, have been largely overlooked by historians; and the Minutes of the PLP's Trade Union Group, held by the current Secretary, Frank Doran MP. Another fascinating source was the Bedwas Navigation Colliery Company Minutes, recording negotiations between the Company and the Federation from December 1936 until January 1938. These were 'saved' by David Sellwood of Caerphilly, and the Bedwas and Trethomas Local History Group have now placed them in the Swansea University Coalfield Collection. To an historian they are worth their weight in gold.

Ness's own books, particularly his first volume of the *'History of the South Wales Miners' Federation'*, and the unpublished Chapters intended for that book, have given particularly valuable insights into the earlier part of Ness's life and work. Local and national newspapers were, of course, a valuable source, as were the memories, sometimes anecdotal, of Ness's friends and acquaintances and Labour Party colleagues, both locally and nationally.

BIBLIOGRAPHY

South Wales Coalfield Collection, Swansea University:

Lodge Records
Arrael Griffin Lodge Minute Books, 1917-1920
Bedwas Lodge Minute Books, 1954-1968
Penallta Lodge Minute Books, 1927-1939

Labour Party Records
Caerphilly Divisional Labour Party (GMC and EC) Minute Books, 1938-1959 (incomplete)
Bargoed Ward Labour Party Minute Book, 1939-1942
Bargoed Labour Party Women's Section Minute Books, 1934-1953
Gelligaer Ward Labour Party Minute Book, 1940-1949
Caerphilly South Ward Labour Party Minute Book, 1950-1957

Colliery Records
Bedwas Navigation Colliery Comp. (1921) Ltd.
Minutes of negotiations with the SWMF, Dec. 1936-Jan. 1938
(recently placed in the collection)

Personal Collections
Crews, W. H.
Edwards, Ness
Evans, Edgar
Nind, W. J.
Price, Leo

Non-Coalfield Archive, Labour Party Records:

Caerphilly Constituency Labour Party Minute Books (GC and EC), 1964-1968, and general correspondence and papers 1960-1968 (National Library of Wales, Aberystwyth)

Bargoed Ward Labour Party Minute Books, 1946-1954 (courtesy of W. H. Coleman)

Welsh Group of the Parliamentary Labour Party Minute Books, 1951-1968 (PLP Office, House of Commons)

Parliamentary Labour Party Trade Union Group Minute Books, 1958-1968 (courtesy of Frank Doran MP)

Interviews conducted with:

Leo Abse
W. H. Coleman
Graham Court
Tam Dalyell
Keith Edwards
Olive Edwards
Maureen Fowler
Dr. Hywel Francis
Jean Gatefield
Baroness Llin Golding
Phil Harries
Margaret Jenkins
Decimer Lawrence
Anne Mitchel
Prof. Allan Rogers
Horace Rowland [deceased]
Peter Slarke
Prof. Dai Smith (by Ben Curtis)
Ken Snell

Newspapers:

Caerphilly Journal
Cymric Democrat
Daily Express
Daily Herald
Daily News Chronicle
Daily Telegraph
Daily Worker
Liverpool Daily Post
Merthyr Express
Plebs Magazine
South Wales Argus
South Wales Echo
The Times
Western Mail

Other Sources:

Ness Edwards personal papers held by Baroness Llin Golding

Photographs and papers regarding Ness Edwards held by Keith Edwards

Various papers relating to Ness Edwards held by Anne Mitchel
Minutes of Caerphilly UDC, 1966 (Glamorgan County Record Office, Cardiff)

Hansard, 1933-1968 (House of Commons)

Great Parliamentary Speeches - Memorable Occasions from the first 16 years of Parliamentary Broadcasting, 1978-1994 (EMI, 1995)

Record: Post Early for Christmas - An appeal in the BBC Home Service, 14 December 1950, by the Postmaster General, Rt. Hon. Ness Edwards (courtesy of Keith Edwards)

Commemorative book about 'Lidice'. Also containing photographs of Buchenwald (courtesy of Alun Jones, St. Martin's School, Caerphilly)

Armed Forces Pension Scheme and preserved pensions - background note (House of Commons Library, January 2005)

Note from Ron Crockett about Ness Edwards's involvement in Caerphilly RFC (August 2005)

Website on the History of the Bedwas Navigation Colliery by David Harris (n.d.)

Recording of speeches by Ness Edwards at the opening of the Aneurin Labour Club and the opening of the Harold Wilson Industrial Estate (courtesy of Baroness Llin Golding)

Published works by Ness Edwards:

The Industrial Revolution in South Wales (London, 1924).

History of the South Wales Miners (London, 1926).

John Frost and the Chartist Movement in Wales (Abertillery, c.1928).

The Workers' Theatre (Cardiff, 1930).

History of the South Wales Miners' Federation (London, 1938).

Caerphilly and its Castles (Caerphilly, 1948).

Is This the Road? (Wrexham and Cardiff, 1956).

BOOKS AND JOURNALS:

Abse, Leo, *Private Member* (London, 1973).

Arnot, R. Page, *South Wales Miners, 2 vols* (Cardiff, 1967 and 1976).

Benn, Tony, *The Benn Diaries, 1940-1990* (London, 1995).

Bernard, Kimberly, 'The National Eisteddfod and the Evolution of the All-Welsh Rule', *North American Journal of Welsh Studies, vol.3,1 (Winter 2003).*

Bevan, Aneurin, *In Place of Fear* (London, 1952).

Bunker, Carol, (comp. by), *Who's Who in Parliament* (London, 1946).

Butt Philip, Alan, *The Welsh Question - Nationalism in Welsh Politics, 1954-1970* (Cardiff, 1975).

Craig, F.W.S., *British Parliamentary Election Results 1918-1949 and 1950-1973* (London, 1977 and 1983).

Craik, W. W., *The Central Labour College* (London, 1964).

Crosland, C. A. R., *The Future of Socialism* (London, 1956).

Crossman, Richard, *The Diaries of a Cabinet Minister, vol.II: Lord President of the Council and Leader of the House of Commons* (London, 1976).

Curtis, Ben, 'The Wilson Government and Pit Closures in South Wales 1964-1970', *Llafur - Journal of the People's History Society, vol.9 (2004).*

Dalton, Hugh, *High Tide and After: Memoirs 1945-1960* (London, 1962).

Eastwood, C. G., *George Isaacs. Printer, Trade-Union Leader, Cabinet Minister* (London, 1952).

Edwards, Ness, 'Review of W. W. Craik, The Central Labour College' in *Welsh History Review* (vol.2 1965).

Felstead, Richard, *No Other Way: Jack Russia and the Spanish Civil War, a Biography* (Port Talbot, 1981).

Foot, Michael, *Aneurin Bevan, 2 vols* (London, 1962 and 1973).

Francis, Hywel, *Miners Against Fascism: Wales and the Spanish Civil War* (London, 1984).

Francis, Hywel, (ed.), *Adult Education in the Valleys: the last 50 years. Report on Llafur Conference, May 1986* (Cardiff, 1986).

Francis, Hywel and David Smith, *The Fed: A History of the South Wales Miners in the Twentieth Century* (2nd edit., Cardiff, 1998).

Griffiths, James, *Pages from Memory* (London, 1969).

Griffiths, Robert, *S. O. Davies - A Socialist Faith* (Llandysul, 1983).

Horner, Arthur, *Incorrigible Rebel* (London, 1960).

Jenkins, Mark, *Bevanism - Labour's High Tide* (Nottingham, 1979).

Jones, Glyndwr G., 'A Caerphilly Childhood, Reminiscences of the years 1930-1940', *Chronicl Caerffili, No. 4* (1977).

Morgan, K.O., *Rebirth of a Nation: Wales 1880-1980* (Oxford, 1981).

Morgan, K.O., *Labour in Power 1945-1951* (Oxford, 1985).

Paynter, Will., *My Generation* (London, 1972).

Price, Emyr, *Lord Cledwyn of Penrhos* (Gwynedd, 1990).

Prothero, Clif., *Recount* (Lancashire, 1981).

Rees, Dylan, 'Morgan Jones, Educationalist and Labour Politician', *Morgannwg, v.xxxi* (1987).

Samuel, Raphael, 'Theatre and Socialism in Britain (1880-1935)' in *Theatres of the Left (1980-1935). History Workshop Series* (London, 1985).

Smith, Dai, *Out of the People: A Century in Labour* (Aberystwyth, 2001).

Smith, Dai, *Wales! Wales?* (London, 1984).

Smith, David, *Aneurin Bevan and the World of South Wales* (Cardiff, 1993).

110

Smith, David B., 'The Struggle Against Company Unionism in the South Wales Coalfield, 1926-1939', *Welsh History Review, VI/3* (1973).

Smith, J. Beverley, (ed.,), *James Griffiths and his Times* (Rhondda, 1977).

Smith, J. G., 'The DEA - Wilson's Economic Revolution?' *Labour History - The Journal of the Labour History Group, 2* (Spring 2004).

Stenton, M. and S. Lees, *Who's Who of British Members of Parliament, 1945-1979, vol.4* (London, 1981).

Swain, F. and C. Williams, (eds.,), *Penallta - A Brief History of the Penallta Colliery in the Rhymney Valley (A project by pupils of Lewis Girls' Comprehensive School, Ystrad Mynach).* (Bridgend, 1994).

Tanner, D., C. Williams and D. Hopkin, *The Labour Party in Wales, 1900-2000* (Cardiff, 2000).

Williams Gwyn A., 'Locating a Welsh Working Class: the Frontier Years', *A People and a Proletariat. Essays in the History of Wales,* edited by David Smith (London, 1980).

Williams, Phil, *The Psychology of Distance* (Institute of Welsh Affairs pamphlet, 2003).

INDEX